Sanchi

Monumental Legacy

Series Editor: Devangana Desai

ARWIND P. JAMKHEDKAR
Ajanta

R. NAGASWAMY
Mahabalipuram

FREDERICK M. ASHER
Bodh Gaya

B.M. PANDE
Qutb Minar and its Monuments

THOMAS DONALDSON
Konark
(Oxford India Paperbacks)

JOSÉ PEREIRA
Churches of Goa
(Oxford India Paperbacks)

M.K. DHAVALIKAR
Ellora
(Oxford India Paperbacks)

GEORGE MICHELL
Pattadakal
(Oxford India Paperbacks)

ANILA VERGHESE
Hampi
(Oxford India Paperbacks)

DEVANGANA DESAI
Khajuraho
(Oxford India Paperbacks)

Monumental Legacy

SANCHI

M.K. Dhavalikar

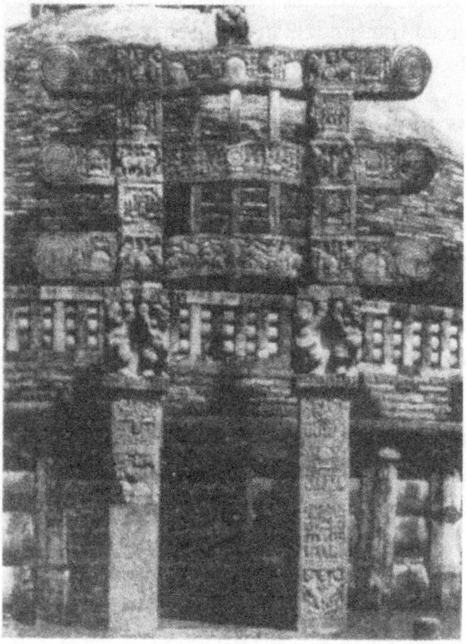

OXFORD
UNIVERSITY PRESS

OXFORD
UNIVERSITY PRESS

Oxford University Press is a department of the University of Oxford.
It furthers the University's objective of excellence in research, scholarship,
and education by publishing worldwide. Oxford is a registered trademark of
Oxford University Press in the UK and in certain other countries

Published in India by
Oxford University Press
YMCA Library Building, 1 Jai Singh Road, New Delhi 110 001, India

First Edition published in 2003
Oxford India Paperbacks 2005
Fourth impression 2015

ISBN-13: 978-0-19-567590-0
ISBN-10: 0-19-567590-8

Typeset by Le Studio Graphique, Delhi 110 017
Printed in India by Replika Press Pvt. Ltd

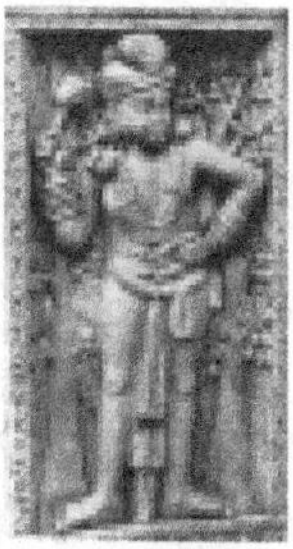

Series Editor's Preface

There are 721 sites on the World Heritage list, as on December 2001, 'inscribed' as properties by the World Heritage Committee of UNESCO. These sites are 'considered to be of outstanding value to humanity', and the preservation of this shared heritage concerns all of us. India has been an active member-state on the World Heritage Forum since 1977, and is one of the countries on the list, with 22 World Heritage Sites. Of these, 17 are recorded as cultural sites, while the rest are natural sites.

I am delighted that the Oxford University Press is publishing brief books on each of the 17 cultural sites, under its series titled Monumental Legacy. So far, the following cultural sites in India have been listed as World Heritage sites:

Ajanta Caves (1983), Ellora Caves (1983), Agra Fort (1983), Taj Mahal (1983), Sun Temple, Konarak (1984), Group of Monuments at Mahabalipuram (1985), Churches and Convents of Goa (1986), Group of Monuments at Khajuraho (1986), Group of Monuments at Hampi (1986), Fatehpur Sikri (1986), Group of Monuments of Pattadakal (1987), Elephanta Caves (1987),

Brihadisvara Temple, Thanjavur (1987), Buddhist Monuments at Sanchi (1989), Humayun's Tomb (1993), Qutb Minar and its Monuments (1993), and the Darjeeling Himalayan Railway (1999).

There is scope, indeed, for recognition of many more Indian sites in future on the World Heritage list. I am sure that as, and when, these are declared as World Heritage Sites, they will be included under the Monumental Legacy Series of the Oxford University Press.

The Oxford University Press, in consultation with me, have invited experts in the field to contribute small books, addressed to general readers, on each of these 17 World Heritage Sites in India. These books, obviously, differ from cheap tourist books and glossy guide books and, at the same time, also from specialized monographs. Their importance lies in the fact they are written by authorities on the subject, to enable visitors to see the monuments in proper perspective.

My sincere thanks to all the authors of the Series and to the editorial staff at the OUP. Their constant support and enthusiasm are much appreciated.

2002 DEVANGANA DESAI

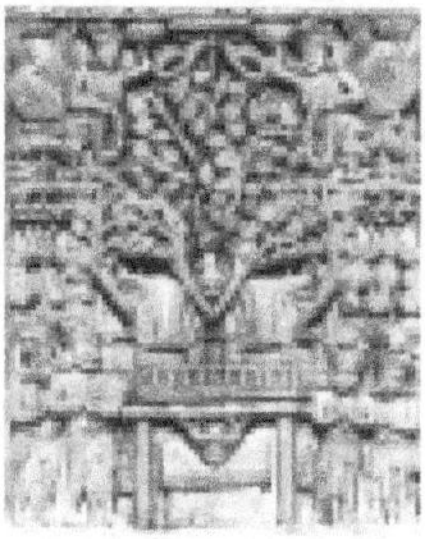

Contents

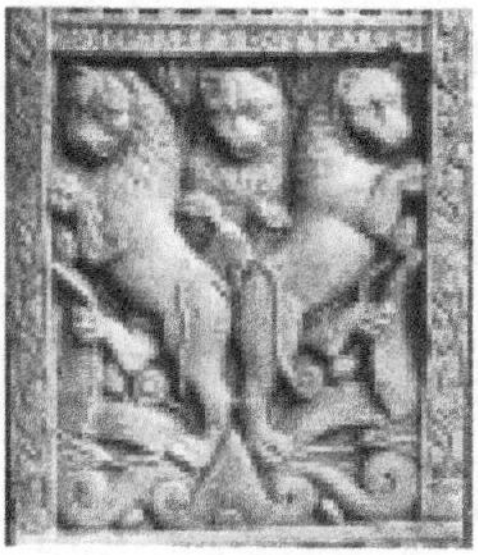

Acknowledgements

I gratefully acknowledge the help received from the following organizations and individuals:

1. Archaeological Survey of India, for reproducing the plan showing Sanchi monuments, plan of the Great Stupa, drawings of the location of panels on the four Gateways of the Great Stupa, and plans and elevations of Stupas 2 and 3.

2. American Institute of Indian Studies, Art and Archaeology Centre, Gurgaon, for supplying black-and-white photographs.

3. Mr P.R. Ahirrao, for supplying colour photographs.

4. Mr Srikant Pradhan, artist, for line illustrations.

5. Mr Sharad Gosavi for computer typing.

6. Librarians of Deccan College and Bhandarkar Oriental Research Institute, Pune.

M.K. DHAVALIKAR

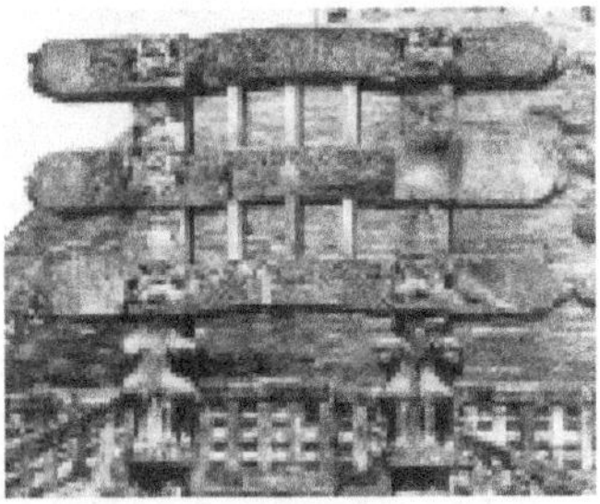

Illustrations

ONE

Historical Background

Sanchi, in central India (latitude: 23°28′ North, longitude: 77°48′ East), has an important group of Buddhist monuments built over a period of 1400 years from the 3rd century BC to the 12th century AD (Figures 1.2, 1.3, and 1.4). These Buddhist monuments are included in the World Heritage list of UNESCO since 1989. Sanchi is situated 9 km south-west of Vidisha which, in pre-Independence days, was known as Bhilsa, and later as Besnagar, but has now been renamed Vidisha, its ancient name.

The region around Vidisha has been the habitat of man from prehistoric times. Prehistoric tools belonging to the different phases of the Stone Age have been discovered at nearby Bhimbetka in a prehistoric cave. Besides, there are numerous rock shelters which were occupied by prehistoric man as is evident from the paintings on their walls. In the second millennium BC, rural farming communities were living here, and at the beginning of the historical period of the 6th–5th centuries BC, at the time of Buddha, the region formed part of the great republic (*maha-janapada*) of Akara (western Malwa).

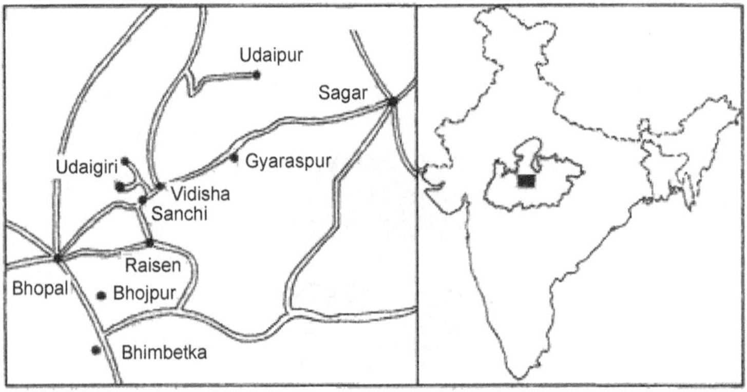

Fig. 1.1 Map showing Sanchi, Madhya Pradesh

Art activity began at Sanchi even before Ashoka (272–232 BC), but it became an important commercial town when he occupied the Mauryan throne at Pataliputra. Agnimitra, the son and successor of Pushyamitra Shunga, shifted the capital here from Pataliputra (present Patna, capital of Bihar) in the 2nd century BC. The Shungas, who ruled after the Imperial Mauryas from 187 BC to 75 BC, have been credited with the revival of Hinduism and are generally branded as the persecutors of Buddhists. This view, however, is based more on literary evidence, and the mere fact that the Shungas revived the *Ashvamedha* sacrifice and built a few Hindu temples has been cited as evidence of their being pro-Hindu and anti-Buddhist. But we have to revise our opinion if we take into consideration the Buddhist edifices which were created during the Shunga period, such as those at Sanchi and Bharhut, which are among the grandest artistic creations in India. Epigraphical evidence from Bharhut clearly mentions that the monument was constructed during the Shunga rule. A Bharhut inscription (No. 108) records the gift of one Chapadevi, the wife of Revatimitra of Vidisha, who probably belonged to the royal family of Central India and may have been very closely connected with the Imperial Shungas—as the suffix 'mitra' of his name indicates. It is therefore clear that Buddhism

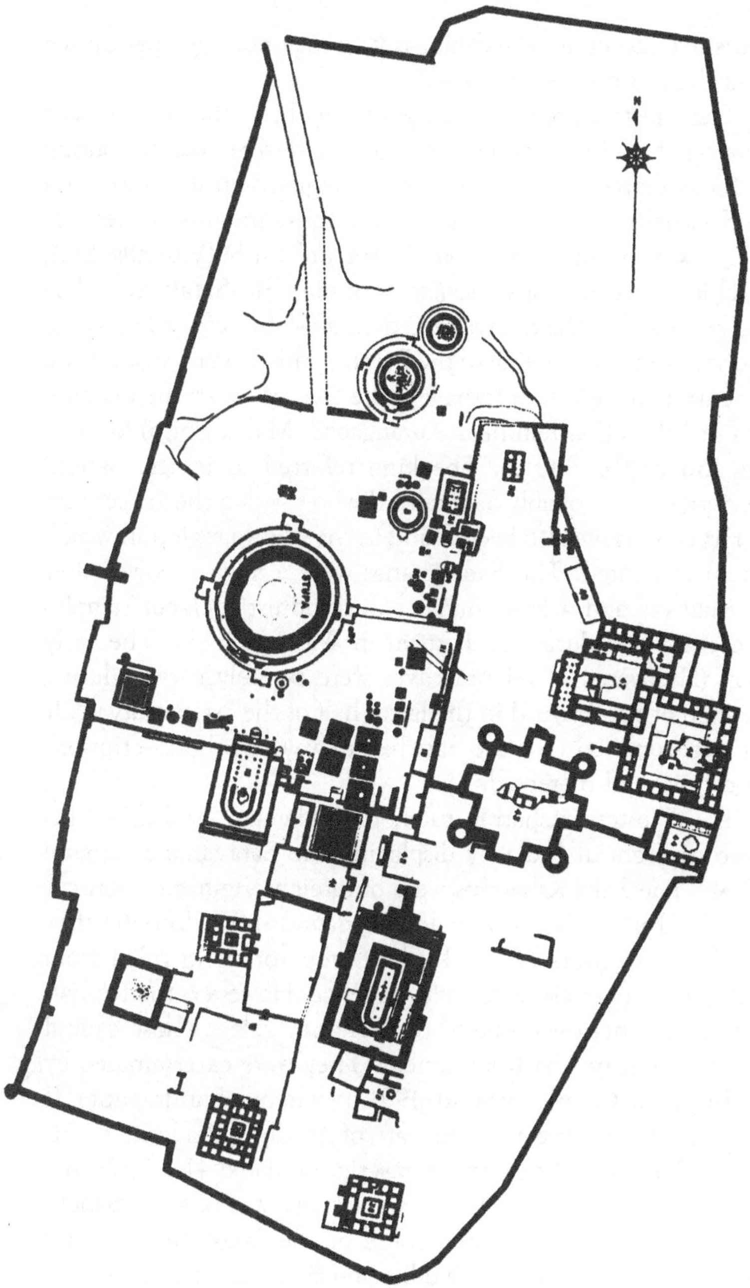

Fig. 1.2 Plan showing monuments at Sanchi, Madhya Pradesh

flourished also under the Shungas who may not have patronised it but did not suppress it either.

The most impressive feature of Sanchi is the magnificent gateways of the Great Stupa (Fig. 1.3) which were executed during the Satavahana domination over this region. An inscription on the Southern Gateway, which is the most impressive, records that "it was the gift of Ananda, the son of Vasithi (*Vasishthi*, Sk.), the chief of the artisans (*aveshanin*) of king Siri-Satakarni." The king belonged to the Satavahana dynasty—also referred to as the Andhras—who, according to the Puranas, ruled over a vast empire in Central and Western India and the Deccan, with their capital at Pratishthan (Paithan near Aurangabad, Maharashtra) for over four and half centuries. The king referred to in the Sanchi inscription was probably Satakarni II who ruled in the 1st century BC. His coins have also been found in the Malwa region in which Sanchi is located. The Satavahanas were a mighty power after the Mauryas and a large number of Buddhist rock-cut temples were excavated during their reign in Western India. The early group (Hinayana) of Ajanta caves were possibly carved during the reign of Satakarni II in the latter half of the 1st century BC. It was in this period that the Sanchi gateways, as the inscriptions suggest, were also erected.

The Western Kshatrap ruler, Rudradaman, established his rule over Central India by displacing the Satavahanas around 150 AD. The Saka-Kshatraps were of foreign origin but soon got naturalized in India, as their Indian names show. Initially they were the governors of the Kushan emperors who ruled from Mathura but later assumed independence. However, the Kushan activity at Sanchi was due to the Kshatrap rulers whose capital was at Ujjain, not far from Sanchi. They were exterminated by the Imperial Guptas around 399 AD when Chandragupta II annexed Malwa (the western part of Madhya Pradesh) to his empire. This is evident from an inscription dated 412–13 on the balustrade of the Great Stupa. Art activity was brisk at Sanchi during the Gupta rule when some of the finest temples and monasteries were built and Buddha and Bodhisattva images were installed. The Gupta period (260–600 AD) has been the Golden

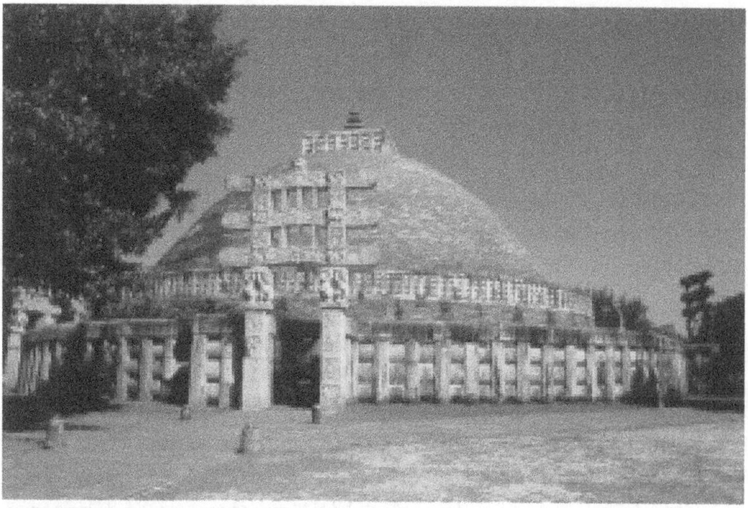

Fig. 1.3 The Great Stupa with gateways

Age of Indian history when remarkable progress was made in every field of human activity.

Buddhism was on the decline in the post-Gupta era from the 7th century AD and only a few buildings were added at Sanchi. The period is marked by internecine conflicts and not much progress could be made. From 1000 AD onwards, Muslim invasions began and the arts also declined. Sanchi, as a Buddhist centre, suffered considerably and came to an end by the 12th century AD.

It is rather enigmatic that the Buddhists should have selected Sanchi for erecting one of their most imposing edifices in the country because the place is nowhere stated to have been associated with Buddha, nor does it figure in Buddhist literature. What is more, even the celebrated Chinese pilgrims, Fa-Hien (399–411 AD) and Hieun Tsang (629–641 AD), who came to India ostensibly to visit Buddhist religious centres, do not make even a passing reference to Sanchi, let alone visit. The question that then naturally arises is: why did Ashoka erect such a magnificent monument at a place which was not associated with the life of the 'Enlightened One'? Probably the only plausible explanation seems to be that Ashoka had married the daughter of a banker of

Vidisha when he was posted here as Viceroy. However, there is a strong possibility of the existence of a Buddhist establishment—may be modest—at Sanchi even before Ashoka. The *Mahavamsha*, a Buddhist text from Sri Lanka, explicitly states that when Mahendra, a son of Ashoka, went to Sri Lanka as a missionary, he halted en route at Vidisha to meet his mother, Devi. She is said to have arranged for his stay in the nearby Chetiyagiri monastery which, in all likelihood, must be Sanchi. When Ashoka became the king, he must have selected the spot for the Great Stupa, when he developed love for Buddhism. Once the *Mahastupa* came up, it was encased in stone by the Shungas, and was embellished with magnificent sculptured gateways during the Satavahana reign. The place was slowly gaining importance and it continued to flourish upto the 12th century AD.

Sanchi was deserted in the 13th century AD and became desolated forever. It was discovered by General Taylor in 1818 who found it in a good state. The monuments were studied in great detail by Alexander Cunningham, James Fergusson and General F.C. Maisey. Sanchi thus attracted the attention not only of antiquaries, but also of treasure hunters as the site was littered with sculptures and carvings. Among those who are responsible for the systematic destruction of the site, mention must be made of one Captain Johnson, Assistant Political Agent at Bhopal, who in 1822 opened the Great Stupa from top to bottom on one side. This caused much damage and as a result the Western Gateway collapsed. He also destroyed Stupas 2 and 3 in parts. Cunningham and Maisey were responsible for damaging the monuments further by their haphazard and badly done excavation in 1851. It may, however, be noted that the only saving grace were the drawings made by Maisey, which were later used by James Fergusson in his book *Tree and Serpent Worship* which was published in 1866. Casts of the Eastern Gateway (Fig. 1.4) were made and sent to some of the principal museums in Europe. Some measures were taken to undo the damage caused by Johnson's digging and the breach was filled by Major Cole. However, large scale repairs were undertaken only by Sir John Marshall, Director General of Archaeology. He also rescued the

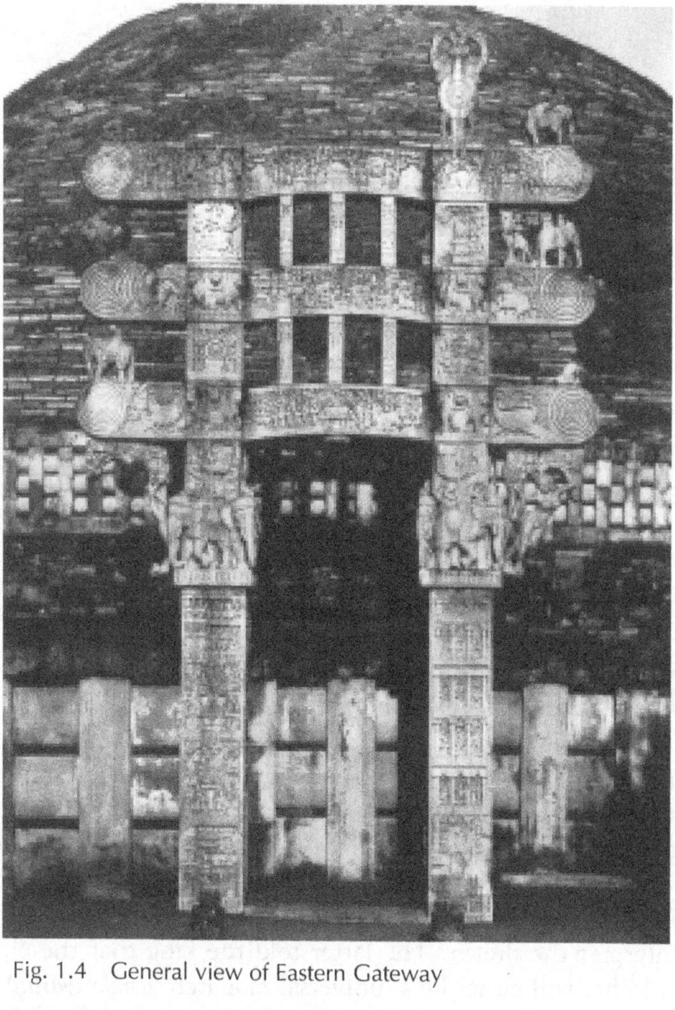

Fig. 1.4 General view of Eastern Gateway

antiquities scattered in the area as well as those recovered from excavations, and established a museum at the site in 1919. Massive conservation measures have been taken since 1947 when the Government of India took over the monuments from Bhopal State, and the Stupas at Sanchi now stand in all their pristine glory.

TWO

Buddhism

Buddha, the founder of Buddhism, was born in the royal family of the Shakyas. He was born in a garden at Lumbini, now in Nepal, just near the Indian border in the Terai region, in 562 BC in his maternal grandfather's house. This locality can be identified because Ashoka (272–32 BC) later set up an inscribed pillar there, recording that it was the birth place of Buddha. When his mother, Maya, was pregnant, she dreamt of a white elephant entering her body. His father, Shuddhodana, then invited the royal astrologer to interpret the dream. The latter told the king that the child born to her will either be a 'universal monarch' (*chakravartin*) or a 'universal teacher', which came true. In course of time Maya delivered, standing below a *shala* (*Shorea robusta*) tree, with god Indra in attendance. The birth of Buddha was an occasion of great joy in the Heaven of Thirty-Three Gods (*Tryastrimsha*). The boy was named Siddhartha, was well educated and married his cousin, a Koliya princess, Yashodhara. With the marriage, the feud between the Shakyas and the Koliyas came to an end.

Buddha

Prince Siddhartha—Gautama was his family name (*gotra*)—was not interested in material pleasures. His father wanted him to become a 'universal monarch' and not a 'universal teacher' and, on the advice of soothsayers, saw to it that the young prince was always engaged in the palace luxuries. To attract him to worldly things, dance and music performances were arranged, but to no avail. Once, in the course of his wanderings through the capital, he saw an old decrepit man, a sick man, and a corpse followed by weeping mourners—which all impressed on him the futility of the material world. But when he saw an ascetic, who was peaceful and happy with inward joy, he was convinced that only by renouncing the world will he be happy. Therefore, one night he left the palace on his horse—Kanthaka—with his personal attendant Chhandaka, but after leaving the city he asked his attendant to go back. According to a Buddhist text, the *Nidanakatha*, the horse died where Gautama left him. He performed the 'Great Renunciation' (*Mahabhinishkramana*) or the 'Great Departure' at the age of twenty-three. On the way, he gave his jewellery to his attendant, cut off his hair with his sword, and tossed his headdress in the sky and said: "If I am to become a Buddha, it will remain in the air". His hair was taken in a casket to heaven (*Tryastrimsha*) and was worshipped by the gods.

Gautama then began to wander, and when he reached Uruvela near Gaya, he performed a severe penance. He was so emaciated that he was reduced to a bundle of bones but his austerities continued. He became a mendicant and wandered along the Nairanjana river where he was offered food by Sujata from a neighbouring village. The same day he went to Bodh Gaya where under a *pipal* tree, Svastika, a grass-cutter, spread grass for him. He practised meditation but was being disturbed by Mara, his cousin, who deputed his beautiful daughters to lure him, and later threatened him by sending his army of demons. But Gautama remained undaunted, continued with his meditation, and became Buddha by gaining 'Enlightenment'. The pipal tree, under which he gained 'Enlightenment', came to be known as the Bodhi tree.

After seven weeks he went to Sarnath, on the outskirts of Varanasi, where he gave his first sermon to his five disciples in the Deer Park (*Mrigadava*). This is the first "turning of the Wheel of Law" (*dharma-chakra-pravartana*), and he began to spread his message among the people. He had many adherents and disciples, and even kings and princes became his followers. He converted the three Kashyapa brothers, the fire worshippers, who were living at Uruvela near Bodh Gaya. He performed many miracles which included walking over water, and driving out a venomous serpent from a temple. These helped him in gaining many adherents. Even Prasenjit, the king of Kosala, his successor Bimbisara, and Ajatashatru of Magadh became his followers. He received many donations, the most lavish of which was that of Jetavana Vihara by Anathapindaka, a rich merchant of Sravasti, who covered the donated land with gold coins. Another noteworthy donation was that by Amrapali, a royal courtesan of Vaishali, who gifted a mango grove, while a bamboo grove (*venuvana*) was donated by king Bimbisara at Rajagriha. Buddha was invited by his father and he therefore visited Kapilavastu, but lived in a grove outside the town. Here he performed the miracle of walking in the air. His father then prostrated before him and presented him the grove of banyan trees. Here he got many adherents—the most important among them being Ananda. At Kapilavastu, he converted his father, his wife Yashodhara, and even his son, Rahul. His wandering was mostly confined to the Ganga valley all around the year, save the four monsoon months. He never, however, visited Sanchi.

Towards the end of his life, at eighty, he died on the outskirts of Kapilavastu, the capital of the Shakyas. According to his wishes, he was cremated and stupas were erected over his ashes at important crossroads. Many more were built later in different parts of the country.

Buddhism spread far and wide in a short period of time because of royal patronage from Ajatashatru and Bimbisara in the 6th–5th centuries BC, and later under Ashoka (272–232 BC). In the earlier period, Buddha was not worshipped in human form. Symbols such as the stupa, the Bodhi tree, his foot prints, and so on, were worshipped instead. Hence we do not see a Buddha image in the early sculptures and on the gateways at Sanchi. The adherents of the early period belonged to the Hinayana sect of Buddhism. But Buddha's images began to be made from 79–80 AD onwards, when followers of the Mahayana sect began to worship Buddha's images. Under the Kushans, in the early centuries of the Christian era, Buddhism spread to Central Asia and China as also to other countries of Asia. But decline set in from the 6th century AD. However, Sanchi continued to be an important Buddhist centre even in post-Gupta times, until the Islamic invasions of the 13th century.

It must be stated that the doctrine of rebirth plays an important role in Buddhism and, accordingly, Buddha is supposed to have had many incarnations in his previous births as man, animal, bird, and so on. These have been described in the *Jataka* stories which number over five hundred. They emphasize the Master's greatness by bringing out his qualities of charity, compassion, benevolence, and so on. A few of the *Jataka* stories have been depicted at Sanchi. In all these stories, Buddha has been described as Bodhisattva which literally means 'being whose characteristic (*sattva*) and aim are "Enlightenment" (*bodhi*)'. Bodhisattva, therefore, is a person who is on the way to becoming a Buddha. There are many Bodhisattvas in the Buddhist pantheon who are quasi-human, quasi-divine, and among these Padmpani (Avalokiteshvara), Vajrapani, Maitreya (future Buddha), and Manjusri frequently figure in Buddhist art.

THREE

The Monuments

The stupas at Sanchi are built over a low hillock, about 90 m high, near the village of the same name. The Vindhyan sandstone of the hill, greyish brown or purple in colour which, though brittle, is rather difficult to carve. The other variety is light grey in colour, and its buff and pinkish varieties are also found. The stone used in the construction of the stupas and other monuments at the site has been quarried from the hill.

Although the stupas have been generally known as the Sanchi stupas, as they are named after the village nearby, it appears that the ancient name of the place was Kakanaya or Kakanava, as is evident from references to it in early inscriptions. This can be identified with the village Kanakheda which is situated at the foot of the hill towards the northwest. It has been referred to as Kakanadabota in the inscriptions of the time of Chandragupta II dated 412–13 AD, which are engraved on the balustrade of the Great Stupa. It is also highly likely that the place Bota-Sriparvata which figures in Bhavabhuti's *Malati-Madhava*, a 6th century play, may be the same as the Sanchi hill.

There is evidence to suggest that some monuments existed at the site in the pre-Ashokan period. According to a story in the *Mahavamsha*, a Buddhist text from Sri Lanka, Ashoka was appointed as the Viceroy of the Mauryan empire in charge of Central India, with headquarters at Vidisha. He is said to have fallen in love with the daughter of a local banker and married her. Two sons, Ujjeniya and Mahendra, and a daughter Sanghamitra were born of her. Ashoka is supposed to have visited a Buddhist vihara at Chetiyagiri nearby which can only be that at Sanchi. When Ashoka succeeded to the Mauryan throne in 272 BC and became the emperor, he built a stupa at Sanchi and also erected a pillar with a lion capital in which four addorsed lions have been shown in a seated posture. It is, however, surprising that Buddha, who was constantly travelling in the Ganga valley in north India, is never once reported to have visited Sanchi. But there must have been a strong community of the adherents of Buddhism in and around Vidisha who were probably responsible for erecting the pre-Ashokan buildings at the site.

It is pertinent to note that when Buddha was breathing his last, he called his favourite disciples, Ananda and Sariputta Moggalana, and told them that after his death (*nirvana*) his body should be cremated, his ashes—his bodily relics—should be distributed, and stupas should be erected over them at the crossroads. This has been narrated in the *Mahaparinibbanasutta*, an early Buddhist text. Accordingly, several stupas were built over Buddha's relics. Seven of the eight original stupas were later opened by Ashoka who, after the Kalinga war, had become a great devotee of the 'Enlightened One' and redistributed the relics among the many stupas—64000 according to a legend—which he himself is said to have built. At Sanchi too, therefore, we can infer that Ashoka built the Great Stupa over the bodily relics of Buddha.

The Buddhist establishment at Sanchi was, no doubt, quite prosperous, as is clear from the numerous inscriptions—nearly a thousand—recording munificent donations. Many of the donors were merchants from nearby Vidisha which is located at the confluence of the Betwa and Beas rivers, and on the trade routes joining Mathura and Pataliputra to West and South India.

Most of the monuments in the complex are built in close proximity to each other and are grouped together on the hill within a walled enclosure, measuring 126×66 m. The circuit wall was built of stone masonry in the 12th century AD, whereas massive embankments of heavy stone masonry, which were constructed for catching drainage from the hill, were probably built in the Shunga period in the second century BC. It was probably during this period that the stupa built by Ashoka was damaged as it was a period of stress and strain following the break up of the Mauryan empire. But shortly thereafter, when the Satavahana rule was established over this region, art activity again picked up and the impressive gateways (*toranas*) of exquisite beauty and grandeur were added. Not much happened during the Kshatrapa rule from c. 100–400 AD, but during the Gupta era in the 5th–6th centuries AD, Buddha images were installed. Temple 17, a gem of a monument, and Temple 40 were constructed during the Gupta period. Several monasteries and temples were erected in the 7th century when Harsha was ruling in north India, and the activity continued upto the 12th century when the Vajrayana sect seems to have dominated, as the presence of images of Vajrasattva, Tara, Marichi, and so on, would suggest. The circuit wall around the plateau, which covers an area of about 400×200 m, was constructed in the 12th century AD. It was in ruins and was therefore heavily repaired by the Archaeological Survey of India at the beginning of the 20th century.

THE GREAT STUPA (*MAHASTUPA*)

The Great Stupa (Stupa I) at Sanchi is the most impressive Buddhist edifice in India, and considering its antiquity and sculptural wealth, it is one of the grandest of man's creations (Fig. 3.1). In its magnificence, it can be compared with the best monuments in the world. Its buff, brownish stone makes it most colourful. It consists of a hemispherical dome (*anda*) with a

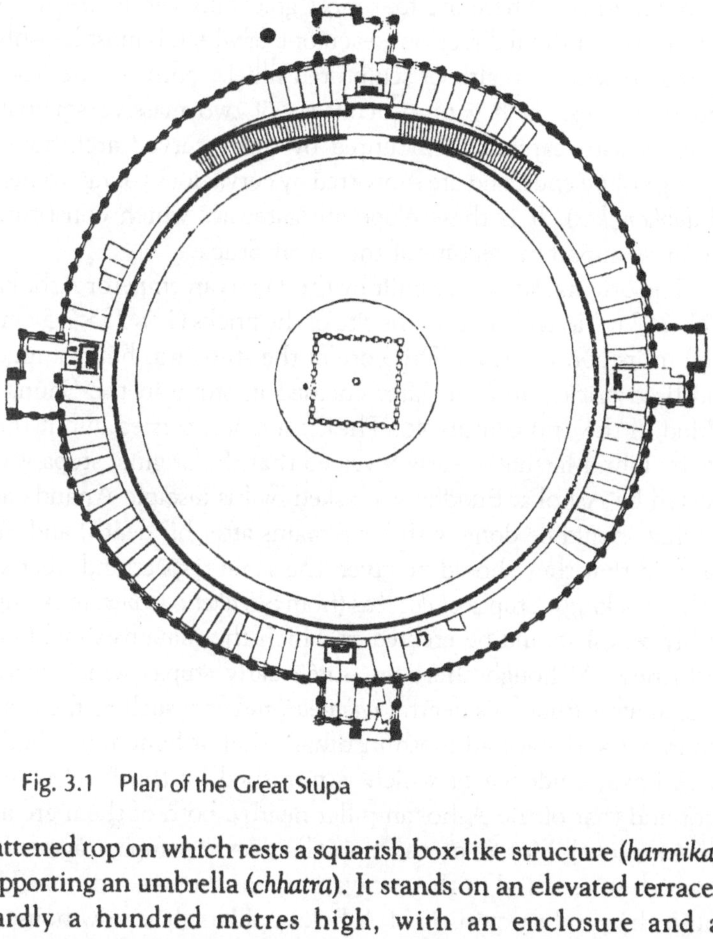

Fig. 3.1 Plan of the Great Stupa

flattened top on which rests a squarish box-like structure (*harmika*) supporting an umbrella (*chhatra*). It stands on an elevated terrace, hardly a hundred metres high, with an enclosure and a circumambulatory path (*pradakshina-path*) which is approached by stairways on either side on the south. The circumambulatory path and the flights of steps have a massive *vedica* rail. Around the stupa on the ground is a procession path. On the ground level is a massive balustrade (vedica) consisting of stone uprights (*thabha*, sk. *stambha*), cross bars (*suchi*), and copings (*ushnisha*), many of which were gifted by donors who have recorded their names in the inscriptions engraved on them. Most of them are from Vidisha and its environs, but a few are from far off places such as Patithana (Paithan) and Bhogavardhan (Bhokardan), both in Maharashtra. There are four most gracefully carved gateways (toranas) in cardinal directions, each one of which is most lavishly decorated with a wealth of sculptured reliefs, both on the front and rear sides. Each gateway consists of two massive squarish uprights with capitals surmounted by three curved architraves having volute ends, and are supported by curvacious young women (*shalabhanjikas*). It is these elaborate gateways which constitute the most important feature of the Great Stupa.

The original stupa was built by the Mauryan emperor Ashoka (272–232 BC) as is clear from the size of the bricks (40×25×7.5 cm) used in its construction. This core of the stupa was built of mud and fired bricks, and was later encased in stone in the Shunga period in the 2nd century BC. The excavation carried out at the site by John Marshall clearly revealed that the original stupa was erected by Ashoka. Buddha was asked by his disciple Ananda as to what should be done with his remains after his death, and he was told that they should be given the same respect and treated as those of kings. Stupas or *dagobas* (from Sk. *dhatu-garbha*, meaning bodily relics) should be erected in which the remains should be enshrined. Although there are some early stupas which were erected after Buddha's death (*maha-pari-nirvana*) such as those at Kumrahar and Vaishali (both in Bihar), that at Sanchi was built by Ashoka, evidence of which is furnished by the level of its floor and that of the Ashokan pillar nearby; both of them are at the same level. Moreover, the umbrella over the stupa, fragments of which were found in the excavation, has the same mirror-like polish that is characteristic of Ashokan pillars. It is now housed in the museum at the site.

The stupa seems to have been reconstructed in the 2nd century BC during the Shunga rule. The original core of the stupa of Mauryan date was encased in stone masonry and the stone terrace and the stairways, with twenty-five steps each at the base, were added. The stone pavement of the Procession Path also belongs to the 2nd century BC. The original balustrade, probably wooden, was replaced by stone balustrade at three places; one at the top, the second around the circumambulatory path at the mid-level, and the last on the ground around the stupa. The Buddha image

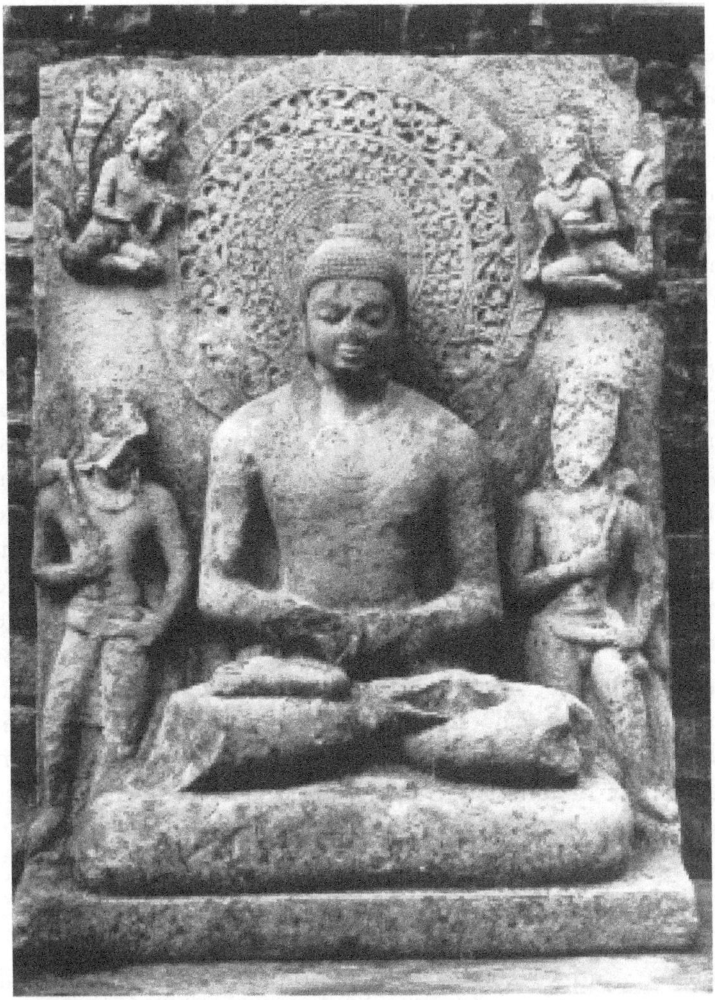

Fig. 3.2 Buddha in meditation (*dhyana-mudra*)

(Fig. 3.2) in the circumambulatory passage near the Southern Gateway, was installed in the 5th century AD. It is badly damaged and weathered. The stone harmika at the top and the umbrella (chhatra) can also be assigned to this phase. These additions increased the overall dimensions of the stupa—the height to 16.2 m and the diameter to 36 m.

The entire dome of the stupa and the terrace were given a very thick layer of concrete over which a fine coat of plaster was applied. This, however, has not survived. The umbrella too was broken; its pieces were found in Marshall's excavation. Fergusson and even Marshall were of the opinion that the renovation work may have taken an inordinately long time—between 50–100 years. This, however, seems unlikely in view of the fact that the flow of munificent donations may have quickened the pace of work. There are several inscriptions on the balustrade which record them.

According to John Marshall, the renovation of the Great Stupa and the additions and alterations made to it were executed during the 2nd century BC when the Shungas were ruling over this region. The Shungas (187–75 BC) who succeeded the Mauryas, have been branded as enemies of Buddhism, and Pushyamitra, the most important king of the dynasty, is blamed for the destruction of several Buddhist monuments in north India. Even though Buddhism may not have received the royal patronage which it enjoyed under Ashoka, this appears to be mere propaganda. It must be noted that even the magnificent Buddhist stupa at Bharhut in central India, which also was embellished with a wealth of sculptures, was erected during the Shunga rule. This only goes to show that the Shungas may not have been devotees of Buddha, but they were not enemies of Buddhism as they have been made out to be.

THE GATEWAYS (*TORANAS*)

The four gateways of the Great Stupa in the four cardinal directions constitute the most impressive artistic creation of its class in ancient India (Fig. 1.4). They were erected during the 1st century BC when the region was under the domination of the Satavahanas (who have been referred to as Andhras by earlier writers). They are all profusely carved with a variety of motifs and narrative panels both on the front and back, and even on the sides of pillars. They are the crowning glory of Buddhist art at Sanchi. They were all erected during a short span of twenty years or a generation, as inscriptions on them clearly suggest. Thus, the inscription on the right pillar of the Western Gateway was donated by the same person as the middle architrave of the Southern Gateway, one Balamitra, who was the pupil of Ayachuda. Similarly, the south pillar of the Eastern Gateway and the north pillar of the Southern Gateway were also the gifts of the same donor, Nagapiya, a banker of Achavada who was a resident of Kurara. The gateways can be placed in the latter half of the 1st century BC on the basis of the evidence of an inscription on the Southern Gateway, which records that it was the gift of Ananda, who was the royal architect of king Satakarni. He can be identified as Satakarni II of the Satavahana dynasty who ruled in the 1st century BC for fifty six years.

All the four gateways are similar in conception and design. Each one consists of two square pillars with capitals, above which are three curved architraves with volute ends. The architraves are separated from one another by squarish stone blocks which are set in pairs above the capitals; in between them are three short uprights and varieties of figures. The vertical uprights too are embellished with dainty carvings. The undersurface of the lowest architrave is adorned with large lotus medallions. All the gateways are so intricately carved that they almost resemble the ivory carvings of the Satavahana period, even stylistically, which have been found in large numbers in the excavations at Begram (ancient Kapisa) in Afghanistan. It must be mentioned in this context that an inscription on the Southern Gateway records that it was executed by the ivory carvers of Vidisha. It is not unlikely that originally the gateways were wooden and were later replaced by those of stone.

The variety of motifs carved on the gateways include Buddhist symbols such as the Bodhi tree, *tri-ratna*, stupa, and so on. As Buddha was not worshipped in human form by the adherents of the Hinayana faith, his worship was symbolical. He was represented by an empty throne, Bodhi tree, foot-prints, and so on. There are motifs such as the eight auspicious symbols (*ashta-mangalakas*), *kalpa-lata* (the wish-fulfilling creeper) or tree (*kalpa-vriksha*), the Wheel of Law (*dharma-chakra*), and so on. The animals include elephants and lions supporting pillars, and elephant and horse riders. Among human figures, mention should be made of corpulent dwarf males (*yakshas*), but the most charming are the nymphs (shalabhanjikas) in the most alluring poses. Above all, there are large narrative panels depicting events from Buddha's life as also the *Jataka* stories which relate Buddha's acts of benevolence, charity, and magnanimity, in his earlier incarnations. All this sculptural wealth constitutes a most precious heritage of humanity. It may incidentally be stated that it is possible to identify a majority of the scenes, but there are quite a few which could be identified only because of similar ones at Bharhut which have label inscriptions.

Of the four gateways of the Great Stupa, the first to be erected was the southern, followed by the northern, eastern and the western. Their relative chronology is suggested by stylistic peculiarities and is corroborated to a great extent by epigraphical evidence. That the Southern Gateway was the first to be erected is evident from its being the main entrance as also by the location of the Ashokan pillar, and is supported by the landing of the stairway on that side. It should be made clear though, that much time did not elapse between the building of the gateways and, therefore, they can all be taken as more or less contemporary.

Of the four gateways, the best preserved is the northern one whereas the southern is considerably damaged. But it must be admitted that they all convey a fair idea of the motifs that have been carved on them. It is interesting to note that they were also painted as the traces of red paint on the Eastern Gateway and the balustrade indicate.

Southern Gateway (Fig. 3.3)

The present approach road leads straight to the Northern Gateway of the Great Stupa, but in ancient times, the main entrance was provided through the Southern Gateway as is evident from the Ashokan pillar just near it. The pillars of the gateway have lion capitals, but the lions are not as majestic as those on the Ashokan pillar. (Fig. 3.4)

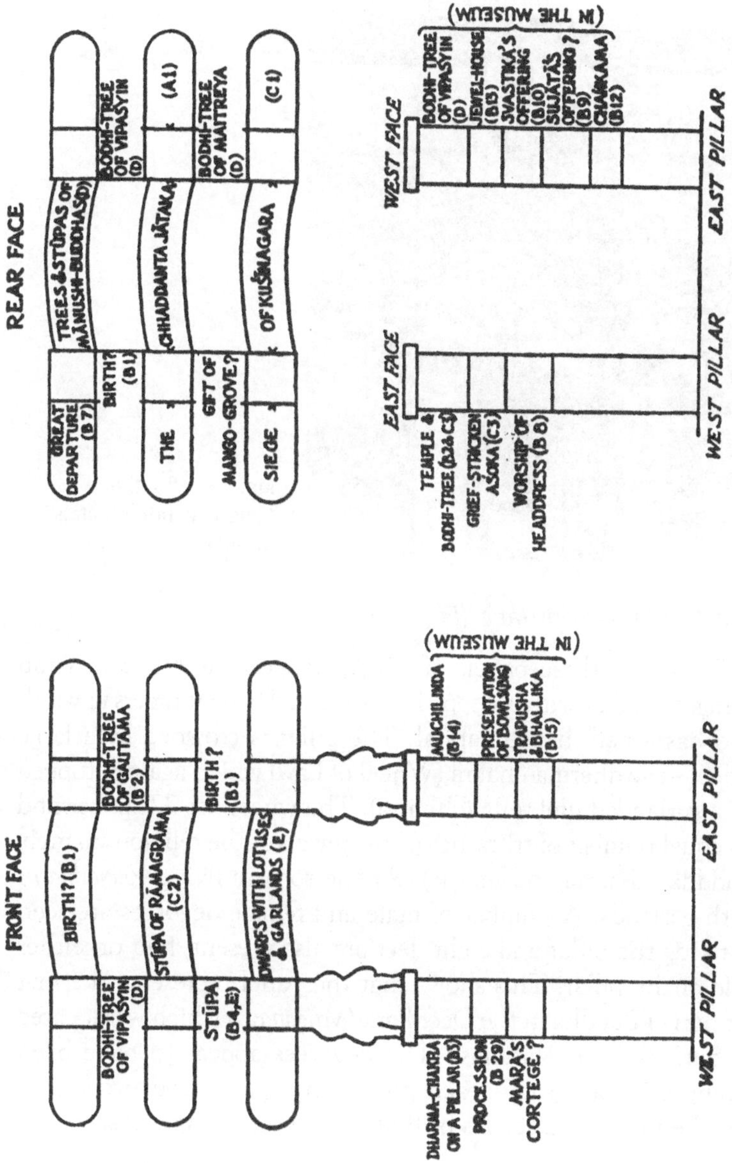

Fig. 3.3 Southern Gateway, location of panels

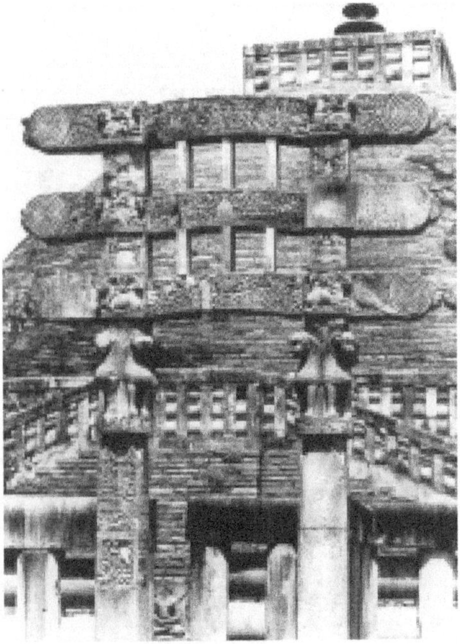

Fig. 3.4 Southern Gateway, lion capitals of pillars

West pillar—front face (Fig. 3.5)

1. There are three panels of which that on the top depicts an octagonal pillar with a stepped, vase-shaped base; it tapers upwards and has a bell-shaped capital. The pillar is crowned by a large wheel—the dharma-chakra (Wheel of Law) which again is topped by a garlanded umbrella (chhatra). The wheel has 32 spokes and an equal number of tri-ratnas (three jewels of the religion, namely Buddha, dharma and *sangha*). At the top are flying *Vidyadharas* with garlands. A number of male and female devotees are seen flanking the pillar and eight deer are also present, four on either side of the pillar. This shows that the panel represents the first sermon of Buddha in the Deer Park (*Mrigadava*) which was located at Sarnath near Varanasi. The devotees appear to have been arranged in four groups, each with a king, queens and attendants, but the first five disciples of Buddha are surprisingly absent.

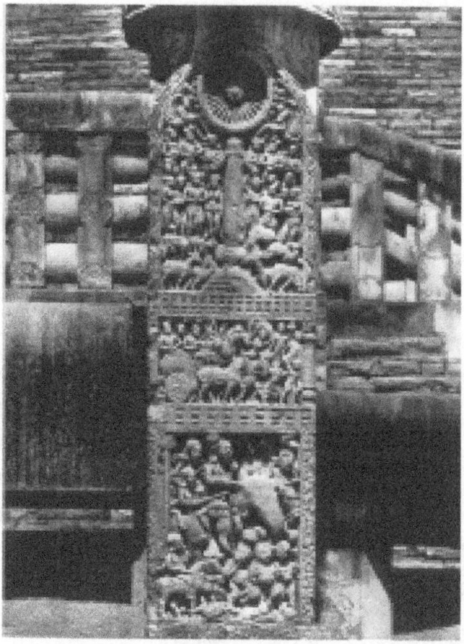

Fig. 3.5 Southern Gateway, west pillar, panels on front face

2. The middle panel is small; it shows a king in a two-horse chariot with his retinue. He may be Ashoka going to worship at the Stupa.

3. There are several figures in this (lowest) panel, the most noteworthy among them being a male and two females riding an elephant, and the other, a male on a horse. Those on the elephant can be identified as Indra, the king of gods, and his two wives. There are also other figures in the retinue and the entire procession is passing through a gateway (torana) with one architrave.

West pillar—east face (Fig. 3.6)

1. & 2. At the top is a shrine with pillars having vase-shaped bases, and a vaulted roof with *chaitya* arches. Inside is seen an empty throne decorated with the tri-ratna motifs. Since this is a Hinayana shrine, the Buddha is not shown in human form but his presence is indicated by the empty throne. Above is a Bodhi

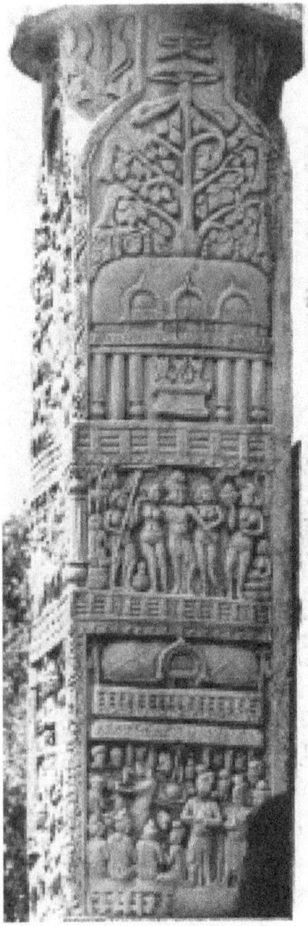

Fig. 3.6 Southern Gateway, west pillar, panels on east face

tree issuing out of the building which may therefore be identified as *vriksha-chaitya.* In the middle panel are a royal couple, with their attendants, who are visiting the shrine. The scene depicts Ashoka's visit to the Bodhi tree, for the king himself speaks in one of his edicts of his visit to the Bodhi tree at Gaya (*samyak sambodhi*). According to a story in the *Divyavadana*, an early Buddhist text, Tishyarakshita, one of Ashoka's queens, was jealous of the Bodhi tree, and because of her machinations the tree began to wither. This she did because of Ashoka's tremendous adoration of the tree. The emperor came to know of this and became very sad. However, the tree again began to blossom because of Ashoka's efforts. He then built a temple over the *vajrasana*, Buddha's seat below the tree which we see in the panel.

A more elaborate depiction of the story is carved on the Eastern Gateway.

3. In this panel, also, there is a building with a vaulted roof having a chaitya arch at the front. There are a number of persons in it. The scene depicts Indra with other divinities in the Heaven of Thirty-Three Gods (Tryastrimsha), worshipping the hair of Buddha. According to a story, Gautama, before becoming Buddha, discarded his princely attire and turban, cut his hair with his sword and tossed it in the sky from where it was taken by the gods to heaven and worshipped. The margin on either side of the

panel is decorated with dainty floral patterns. An inscription records that the carving was done by the ivory carvers of Vidisha. An interesting feature of this panel is that the artist has attempted to obtain a true perspective by recessing the figures at the top and at the same time diminishing their size as they go backwards.

West pillar—west face

It is carved with a huge curved lotus stalk adorned with fruits, flowers, and gem-set necklaces with pendants of auspicious symbols (ashta-mangalakas) as well as human figures, some of which are musicians. Wild animals like lions, too, are present. The entire space is filled with these motifs.

East pillar—front face

The present east pillar is a new replacement. The original, which is in the site Museum, is carved with the panels described below.

1. The top panel of the right pillar portrays the story of Nagamuchalinda. Buddha, after attaining enlightenment, was once travelling, when there was a very strong storm and rain. The Naga king, Muchalinda came there and protected Buddha by holding his seven hoods over his head. In many panels Muchalinda *naga* is shown with cobra hoods over his head.

2. In the middle panel we see the offering of alms bowls. According to a story, two merchants, Trapusha and Bhallika, offered food to Buddha but he had no bowl. He was then offered four bowls, one each by the four *Lokapalas*, who are the guardian deities of directions similar to the *Dikpalas* of the Hindu pantheon. In the panel, only Indra, who was one of the Lokapalas, can be identified on account of the presence of *Panchashikha.*

3. In the lowest panel a bullock cart, with persons, is shown passing through a village. It has been identified with the village Uruvela and the persons in the cart are the merchants Trapusha and Bhallika.

East pillar—west face

1. *Bodhi tree of Vipashyin*

Vipashyin is one of the seven Manushi Buddhas who are the immediate predecessors of Gautam Buddha. They are usually depicted in a group but sometimes individually also. They are distinguished by their distinctive trees. They are: *Patali* (*Bignonia shaveolus*) of Vipashyin: *Pundarika* of Shikhin; *Shala* (*Shorea robusta*) of Vishvabhu; *Shirisha* (*Acacia sirisa*) of Krakuchchhanda; *Udumbara* (*Ficus glomerata*) of Kanakamuni and *Nyagrodha* (*Ficus indica*) of Kashyapa. An excellent illustration of the Manushi Buddhas and their trees has been painted at Ajanta (Cave 17). Sanchi being a Hinayana establishment, they are not shown in their human forms, but are represented by their trees. It is noteworthy that they are shown quite prominently along with the stupas on the middle architrave of the Northern Gateway and the back of the top architrave (north end) of the Eastern Gateway, as also on the top architrave of the Western Gateway where in addition to the Bodhi tree (*nagapushpa*) of Maitreya, the future Buddha is also present.

2. *Jewel house*

This carving, depicting the jewel house, is presently in the museum. Legend has it that it was built by the gods near the Bodhi tree where Buddha is supposed to have lived for a week reciting the *Abhidharma Pitaka*, a Buddhist text.

3. *Svastika's offering*

A grass cutter, named Svastika, offered a bundle of grass to Buddha and spread it under the Bodhi tree for him to sit upon. This event is illustrated in the panel.

4. *Sujata offering food*

This is quite a common motif in Buddhist art. Buddha was meditating under the Bodhi tree and went without food during the penance. When he attained Enlightenment, he was offered a porridge of rice and milk by Sujata, the daughter of the chieftain of Uruvela. This panel is presently housed in the Museum. A better representation is seen on the middle architrave (rear face) of the Northern Gateway.

5. *Lowest panel—Chankama*

Chankama is the promenade where Buddha walked to and fro. After attaining Enlightenment he spent four weeks near the Bodhi tree. Of these, the third week he spent in walking along the promenade (chankama). This panel is also in the Museum.

Southern Gateway

Front face—top architrave (Fig. 3.7)

The panel is reminiscent of Gajalakshmi, the goddess of wealth and prosperity of the Hindu pantheon, as she is shown standing on a full blown lotus and is being bathed by elephants flanking her; she also holds a lotus in her right hand. Other spaces in the panel are filled by lotus leaves and flowers with birds perching on them. It is tempting to identify her as Gajalakshmi, because she is a Buddhist and Jaina goddess as well. The panel can, however, be connected with 'Nativity'—the birth of Buddha. Lotus is associated with miraculous birth, and therefore the panel is identified as symbolizing 'Nativity'. This contention is also supported by Buddhist literature for, according to the *Lalita-Vistara*, at the time of Buddha's birth two *Nagas* (elephants) in the sky miraculously bathed the infant Buddha with two streams of water, one cold and the other warm. Since Buddha is not shown in anthropomorphic form in the Hinayana establishment at Sanchi, they depicted his mother.

The architraves have volute ends (Fig. 3.8). On either end are animal riders and in between the architraves are squarish blocks carved with the Bodhi tree, a stupa, and the Nativity motif. The uprights in between the architraves are missing.

Front face—middle architrave (Fig. 3.7)

This large panel is entirely occupied by the story connected with Ashoka's visit to the stupa at Ramagrama. According to the story, emperor Ashoka is said to have opened seven out of the eight original stupas in which Buddha's bodily relics were enshrined. He desired to distribute them among the stupas which he was going to build. But he could not get those in the stupa at

Ramagrama because it was very zealously guarded and worshipped by the Nagas. In the centre of the panel we see a stupa which is being approached by Ashoka in a chariot, accompanied by his retinue, some on horses and elephants, and his army. There are no women in it. On the left are shown the Nagas of Ramagrama with Naga hoods on their heads. Their females are seen worshipping the stupa. They have a single Naga hood over their head, but the males have five. On the left, two Naga couples are standing in water, their abode. On the extreme left is a couple riding horses. The inscription on the dome of the stupa records that the architrave was the gift of Balamitra who was a pupil of Ayachuda (Arya Kshudra)—the preacher of Law (dharma).

In between the middle and lowest architraves, on the left, is a squarish panel carved with a stupa, and on the right is the Birth of Buddha (Nativity).

Front face—lowest architrave (Fig. 3.7)

The panel depicts dwarfs with lotuses and garlands which is quite a common motif in early Buddhist art, and its excellent illustrations occur in Western Indian caves and in the art of Amaravati. In it, male and female dwarfs are shown bearing garlands and huge lotus stalks are shown issuing out of their mouths. The space in between is filled by flowers, usually lotuses, leaves and even lotus creepers.

To the left of the above is a couple riding a goat-like animal, a mythical creature, and a similar carving can be seen on the corresponding right end. By its side is a beautiful peacock beyond which is the volute end.

Exactly in the middle of both the pillars, on the left and right, are four carved lions standing back to back, in the same way as they occur on the Ashokan pillar at the site. However, they betray inferior workmanship as compared to those on the Ashokan pillar despite the fact that they are in the Mauryan tradition. They look lifeless and lack the vigour of those on the pillar at the site. This is probably due to the fact that they were copied from wooden prototypes.

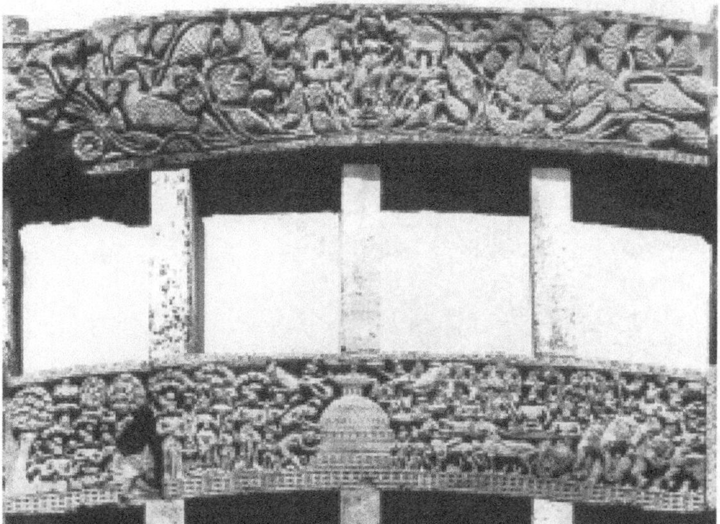

Fig. 3.7 Southern Gateway, front face, panels on architraves

Southern Gateway—back

Top architrave

1. On the extreme left is the Great Departure. When Buddha decided to give up the luxurious royal life, his father Shuddhodana tried to divert his mind with dance and music performances. But he was convinced of the futility of it all, and one night left the

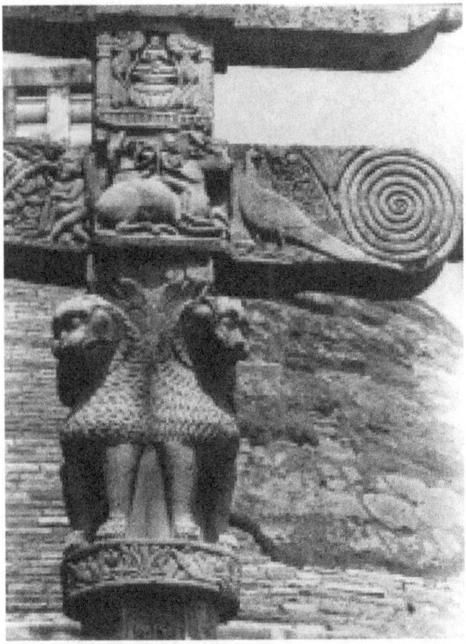

Fig. 3.8 Southern Gateway, front face, panels on eastern end

palace with his horse Kanthaka, and his personal attendant, Chhandaka, to search for Enlightenment. After crossing Anoma, he sent Chhandaka and his horse back. This event is known as the 'Great Departure' in which the horse is shown without a rider. A better illustration of this event is carved on the Eastern Gateway.

2. The middle portion of this architrave is occupied by the trees and stupas of Manushi Buddhas who have already been referred to. In the panel we see four trees and three stupas only, obviously because of limitations of space. The trees can be identified. They are: (1) Shirisha (*Acacia sirisa*) of Krakuchchhanda, on the extreme left; (2) Udumbara (*Ficus glomerata*) of Kanakamuni; (3) Nyagrodha (*Ficus Indica*) of Kashyapa; and finally (4) Pipal (*Ficus religiosa*) of Shakyamuni (Buddha). The aerial roots of the banyan tree are very distinctly shown, as are the leaves of the Pipal tree.

In between the top and middle architraves, the squarish panel on the left shows the Nativity scene and on the right is the Bodhi tree of Vipashyin.

Back—middle architrave—Chhadanta Jataka

The *Jatakas* narrate the stories of past incarnations of Buddha. There are over five hundred *Jataka* stories and among these the most favourite among artists is perhaps the *Chhadanta Jataka*; this can be found from the 2nd century BC onwards at several sites of Buddhist art. It is a tale which delineates the charity and compassion of Buddha. According to the story, Bodhisattva was born as a six-tusked royal elephant, and lived near a lake in the Himalayan region. He had two wives, Mahasubhadda and Chullasubhadda. The latter, who was younger, was very jealous of the former who she thought was favoured by the husband. She therefore wanted to teach him a lesson and prayed to Pratyeka Buddha asking to be born as a beautiful maiden, married to the king of Varanasi, so that she could take revenge. Her prayer was answered and she was born again and became the queen of the king of Varanasi. She became the king's favourite and forced the king, under the pretext of illness, to commission a hunter, Sonuttara, to bring her the tusks of the elephant. The hunter wounded the elephant, but because the elephant was Bodhisattva, full of compassion and charity, he allowed the hunter to cut and take away his tusks. When the tusks were presented to the queen, she fainted and died of remorse.

This story, full of pathos, brings out some of the great qualities of Bodhisattva, and has been very artistically and effectively delineated on the Southern Gateway. The royal elephant is shown with three tusks on one side and he appears four times in the panel. On the extreme left he is enjoying himself in a lotus pond in the company of his wives, who are shown to be smaller than him. There are elephants holding an umbrella and fly whisks over him which indicate his royal status. In the central part he is in the Nyagrodha forest. At the right end he is alone in the forest, where the hunter, who hides himself behind rocks, shoots an arrow, wounding the elephant. The composition of the panel is remarkable; the treatment of the elephants and forest is very sensitive, and hence the panel is extremely effective. This becomes evident when it is compared to those on the Northern and Western Gateways which depict the same *Jataka* story. It is a masterpiece which is unparalleled in early Indian art so far as the extent of treatment and unity is concerned. It displays a very fine sense of line and rhythm which comes of sheer love of beauty. Its delicate refinement distinguishes it from others, particularly those on other gateways.

In the space between the middle and lowest architraves, the squarish panel on the left shows the gift of a mango grove and on the right is the Bodhi tree of Maitreya.

Back—lowest architrave—siege of Kushinagara

After Buddha's death (maha-pari-nirvana) at Kushinagara (present Piprahwa, Basti District, UP) which was the capital of the Mallas, there was a fight for Buddha's ashes. The Mallas had taken possession of the bodily relics of Buddha after his cremation and were not ready to distribute them. There were, in all, seven more claimants who wanted a share of the ashes. They were: (1) Ajatashatru of Rajagriha, (2) the Shakyas of Kapilavastu, (3) the Bulis of Alakappa, (4) the Koliyas of Ramagrama, (5) the Mallas of Pava, (6) the Lichchhavis of Vaishali, and (7) a Brahmana of Vethadvipa. One wise man, Drona, then mediated and pacified them and divided the ashes into eight portions. They all then took their share, went back to their capitals, and erected stupas over the ashes. These eight original stupas were located at Rajagriha, Vaishali, Kapilavastu, Alakappa, Ramagrama, Vethadvipa, Pava, and Kushinagara.

The scene carved on the Southern Gateway depicts only the fight between the different tribes and the Mallas, but has been delineated very graphically. In the centre we see a fortified town with armies ranged on either side. There are elephants, chariots, horsemen, and foot soldiers with bows and arrows, spears, clubs, and so on. Even minute details of fortification, such as the ditch and lotuses in it, are shown. Different standards, flags, and ensigns are clearly seen. Varieties of arms and elephant trappings are noteworthy. The panel gives us a very good idea as to what an ancient Indian town looked like. It was carved by the ivory carvers of Vidisha, as the inscription on it records, and they have carved it as intricately as they would carve on ivory.

Top architrave—back-west end

At the top are animal riders and on the right the story of the 'Great Departure' continues. It depicts a royal person on a horse with attendants holding an umbrella over his head and a fly whisk.

Between the top and middle architraves is shown a stupa with a tree emerging from it, which can be identified as *Bignonia* of Vipashyin, a Manushi Buddha. There are worshippers flanking it.

The middle architrave has what look like bull riders and on the right the *Chhadanta Jataka* continues.

In between the middle and the lowest architraves is the Bodhi tree (Nagapushpa) of Maitreya, the future Buddha.

On the lowest architrave the story continues, and on the squarish block are elephant riders. Below is the lion capital.

Top architrave—back-east end

There are animal riders—couples on bulls—and between this block and the volute end is a horse which can be identified as Kanthaka, and the person standing before him as Chhandaka; the scene therefore signifies the 'Great Departure' (Mahabhinishkramana) of Buddha from the palace in search of attaining enlightenment.

On the squarish block between the top and middle architraves is carved a lotus creeper with flowers and leaves.

The left end of the middle architrave has a volute and by its side is seen an elephant which is partly broken. This, however, is the continuation of the *Chhadanta Jataka* in which the royal elephant is said to have 84,000 elephants in his herd.

The squarish block at the bottom, between the middle and the lowest architraves, is carved with a stupa out of which emerges a Bodhi tree. It may be the tree of some Manushi Buddha, but it cannot be clearly identified. It may even be vriksha chaitya—the shrine of the Bodhi tree.

The lowest architrave has the continuation of the story of the siege of Kushinagara, while the squarish block shows two elephants, one seated and the other standing.

Eastern Gateway (Fig. 3.9)

As in the case of Northern Gateway, this gateway too was standing *in situ* and there was therefore no need to reconstruct it. But it had already lost some of its ornamentation. Thus some of the shalabhanjikas between architraves, the dharma-chakra, the tri-ratna, the yakshis, and the blocks between the uprights in the architraves are missing. The elephant capitals deserve special attention. Four elephants—rather their hindparts—are joined together; they are richly caparisoned with jewelled bands with auspicious pendants around their foreheads, and large bead strings with bells. Their mahouts hold goads in their hands, and one of them holds a banner fluttering atop a shaft which is crowned by a tri-ratna. Palmettes are in the background.

South pillar—front

1. *Chankama (Fig. 3.10)*
We see two rows of votaries, one at the top and the other at the bottom, divided by a broad band which represents chankama, the promenade where Buddha walked. The panel is identical to that on the Southern Gateway. It can be identified only because of a similar one at Bharhut which has a label inscription.

2. *Bodhi tree (Fig. 3.10)*
The panel depicts a shrine in the middle in which there is a tri-ratna over a pedestal, and from its roof emerges a Bodhi tree which is flanked by small mango trees. On either side are two worshippers each, and above there are flying *kinnaras* with bird-like bodies and holding garlands in their hands. This panel

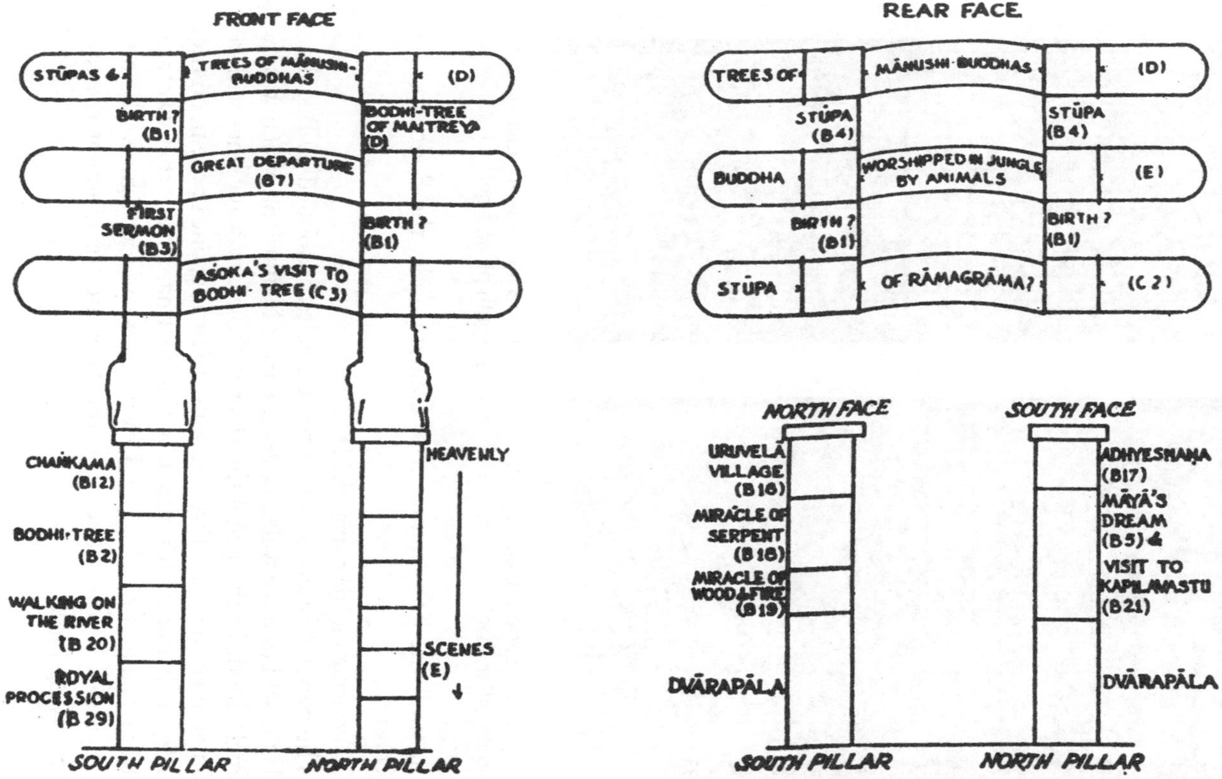

Fig. 3.9 Eastern Gateway, location of panels

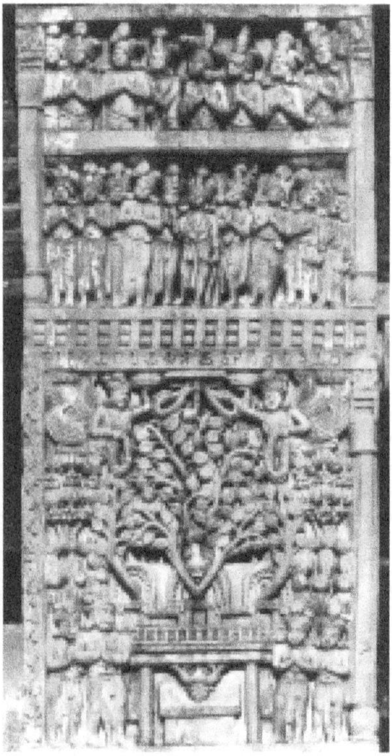

Fig. 3.10 Eastern Gateway, south pillar, front

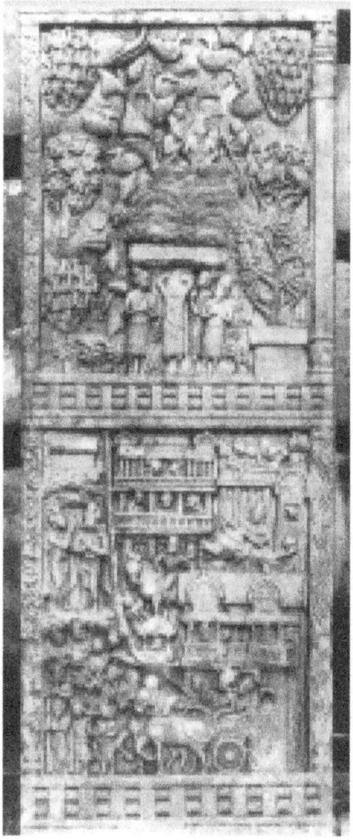

Fig. 3.11 Eastern Gateway, south pillar, front

signifies the Enlightenment of Gautam under the Bodhi tree at Gaya.

3. *Walking on river (Fig. 3.11)*

The panel delineates one of the miracles performed by Buddha. He is said to have walked over the river Nairanjana which was in high flood. In the panel the river is shown by wavy lines with a small boat in which three persons are sitting; one of them, on the left, with oar in his hands is the boatman; the other two are Kashyapa and his disciple. Down below are four figures who are impressed by the miracle; on the sides are trees, and at the top are flying birds.

4. *Royal Procession (Fig. 3.11)*
This is a common motif at Sanchi in which a royal personage is shown passing through a city gate in a chariot followed by a retinue, while citizens watch from their houses.

South pillar—north face

All the three panels on this side of the pillar represent one story: The conversion of the Kashyapas.

1. In the top panel (Fig. 3.12) the village of Uruvela is very graphically depicted. We see villagers doing their daily chores; their small huts, the cattle and the lotus pond are all shown in great detail.

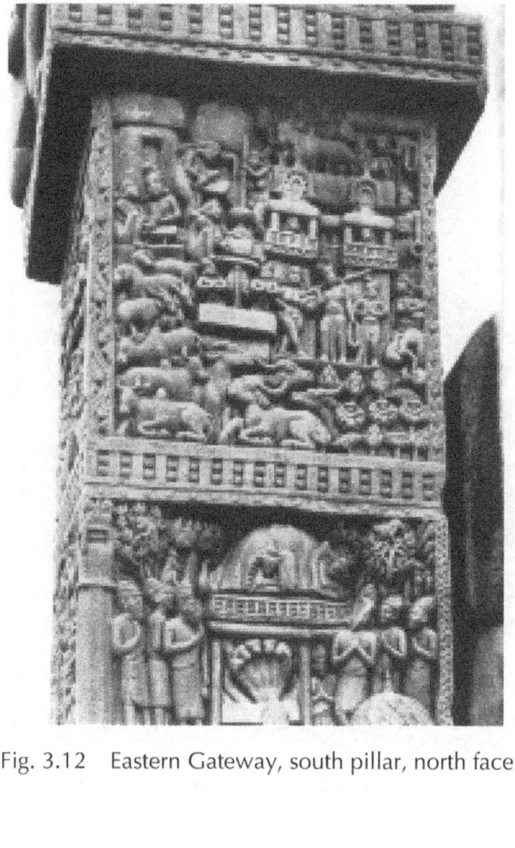

Fig. 3.12 Eastern Gateway, south pillar, north face

2. In this panel (Fig. 3.13) there are three anchorites who can be identified from their matted looks. They are shown standing next to a temple inside which is a five-hooded cobra. By the side is a pedestal which is Buddha's seat. The panel portrays one of Buddha's miracles. According to the story, Buddha once wanted to stay in Kashyapa's hermitage in a fire temple for a night. But it was already occupied by a mighty, venomous cobra. When Buddha went in, the cobra attacked him with fire and smoke, but was subsequently defeated and took refuge in Buddha's bowl. In the panel, the ascetics are seen standing in adoration. In the foreground, on the right, is the hut of Kashyapa which is covered with leaves (*parnakuti*); nearby is a fire altar. On the left is the Nairanjana river from which ascetics are drawing water, probably to put out a fire, and one is bathing.

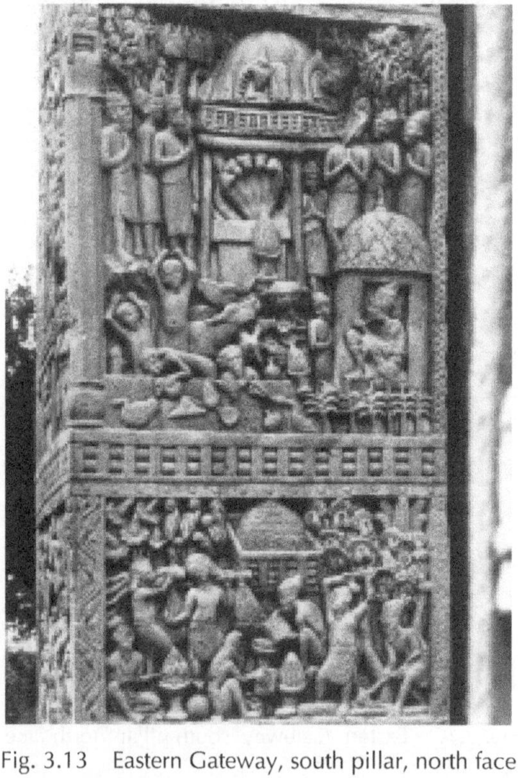

Fig. 3.13 Eastern Gateway, south pillar, north face

3. The panel (Fig. 3.13), like the preceding two, depicts yet another miracle of Buddha related to the conversion of Kashyapa. After the miracle of the fire temple in the preceding panel, the *brahmanas* wanted to perform a sacrifice, but the fire could not be lit as the wood could not be split, and oblations could not be offered without Buddha's consent. At the bottom in the centre, a brahmana is shown holding an axe for splitting wood, but cannot do it without Buddha's permission. Another person is fanning the fire, but it does not burn until Buddha permits. The third one is holding a spoon for oblations. They could perform the sacrifice only after Buddha permitted them, to do so.

4. *Dvarapala* (Fig. 3.14): the guardian (*dvarapala*) is shown standing in a slightly flexed posture with the left hand akimbo and the right holding a flower. He wears a short *dhoti* reaching the knees; its front pleats are left loosely dangling between the legs. He

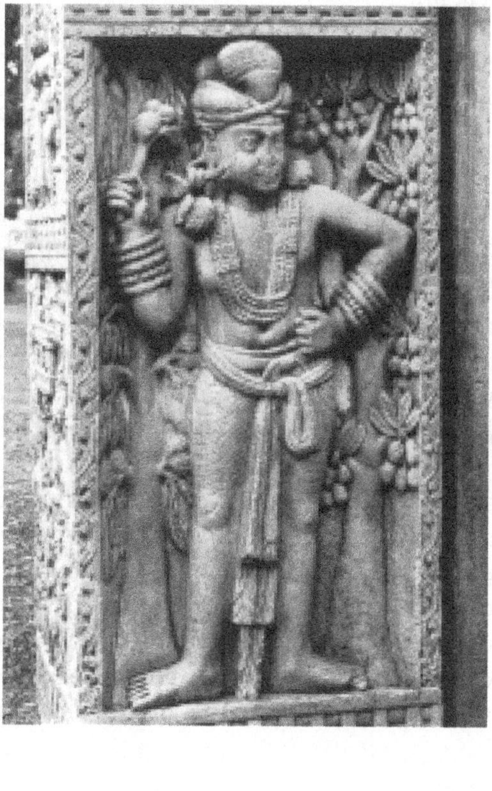

Fig. 3.14 Eastern Gateway, south pillar, north face

wears a number of heavy bracelets and a multi-stringed necklace with spacers; the ear ornaments too are heavy. His turban is wound around the head in such a way that the mass of hair is combed into a ball which is gathered in the headdress and is seen protruding on the top of the head. At the back are fruit-laden trees. There are similar guardians on other gateways also.

South pillar—south face (Fig. 3.15)

It is elegantly carved with a huge lotus creeper which issues out of the crocodile mouth of an elephant with a fish tail. Geese are interspersed very skillfully with lotus flowers and leaves.

North pillar—north face

This face is carved with large lotus medallions set in a vertical band which is flanked by lotus creepers with flowers along the margin.

North pillar—front face (Fig. 3.16)

The panel depicts the six heavens of the gods (*devalokas*) in which passions remain unquenched. From the bottom upwards they are: (1) the heaven of the four great kings—the guardians of four quarters (*Lokapalaschaturmaharajikas*); (2) the Heaven of Thirty-Three Gods (Tryastrimsha) over whom Shakra presides; (3) the heaven over which *Yama*, the god of death, rules, where there is no day or night; (4) the *Tushita* heaven, where Bodhisattvas are born before they appear on earth as the saviours of mankind, and where Maitreya, the future Buddha, resides; (5) the heaven of *Nirmanarati*; and (6) the heaven of the *Parinirmita-vashavartin* gods.

All these six heavens are shown like the six stories of a building supported by plain octagonal pillars with capitals of winged animals seated back-to-back. The two lower panels are much damaged but the remaining four are intact. They are occupied by royal figures of gods with attendants. The panels are therefore taken to represent heavenly scenes. This assumption is to some extent supported by the central figure in three of the seven storeys who holds a thunderbolt in his right hand and may, therefore, be

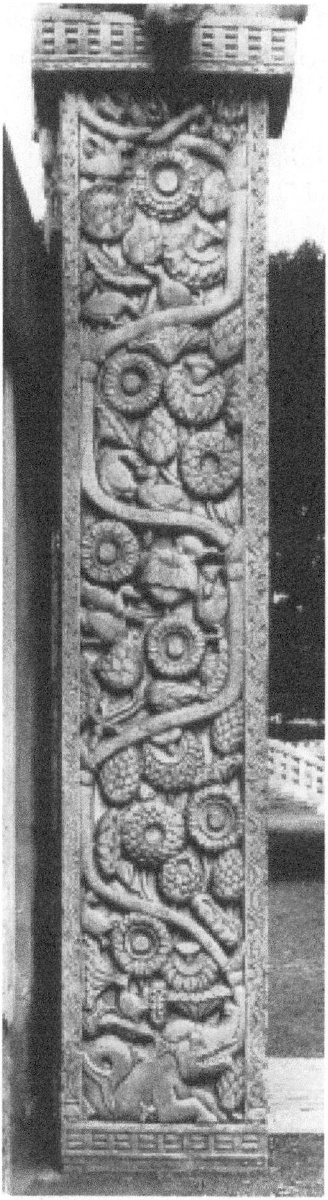

Fig. 3.15 Eastern Gateway, south pillar, south face and north pillar, north face

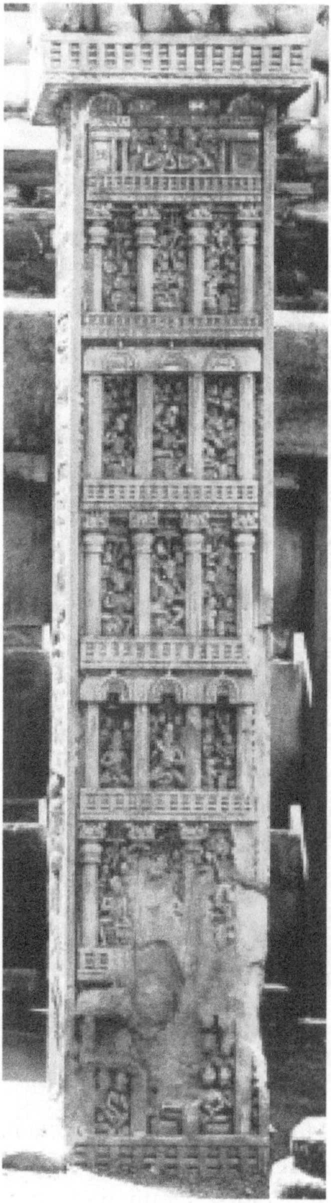

Fig. 3.16 Eastern Gateway, north pillar, front face

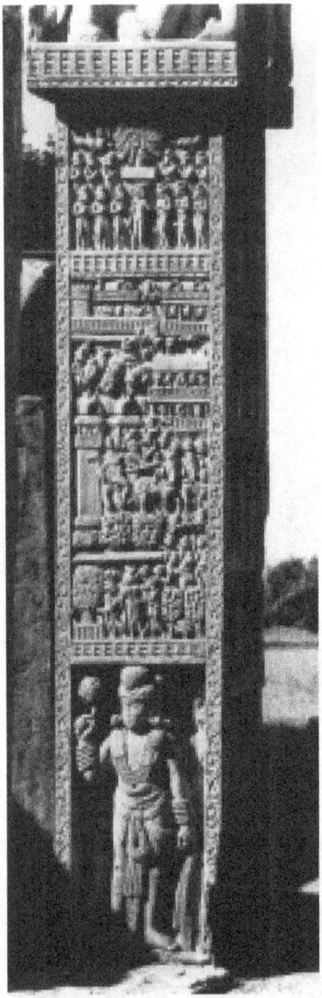

Fig. 3.17 Eastern Gateway, north pillar, south face

Indra (Shakra). The panel is very intricately carved and could be the work of ivory carvers.

North pillar—south face (Fig. 3.17)

1. *Adhyeshana*

The top panel shows the Bodhi tree on a pedestal with a number of worshippers on either side and below. This may represent the *adhyeshana*. According to a story, Buddha went from the *rajayatana* tree to the goat-herd's mango tree as he had not decided whether he would preach the Truth realised by him. Therefore the gods, led by Brahma, requested him to expound it for the benefit of the people. In the panel the two central figures in the lower row may be Brahma and Indra talking to each other.

2. *Maya's dream*

Just below is the scene showing Maya's dream. Buddha's mother, Maya, is shown sleeping in the palace, dreaming of a white elephant entering her body. Persuaded by the gods in the Tushita heaven, Bodhisattva descended on earth in the form of a white elephant which Maya, the queen of Shuddhodana, saw entering her body in a dream. The dream was interpreted by royal astrologers as very auspicious, signifying that a 'universal monarch' or a 'universal teacher' would be born to her. The dream came true.

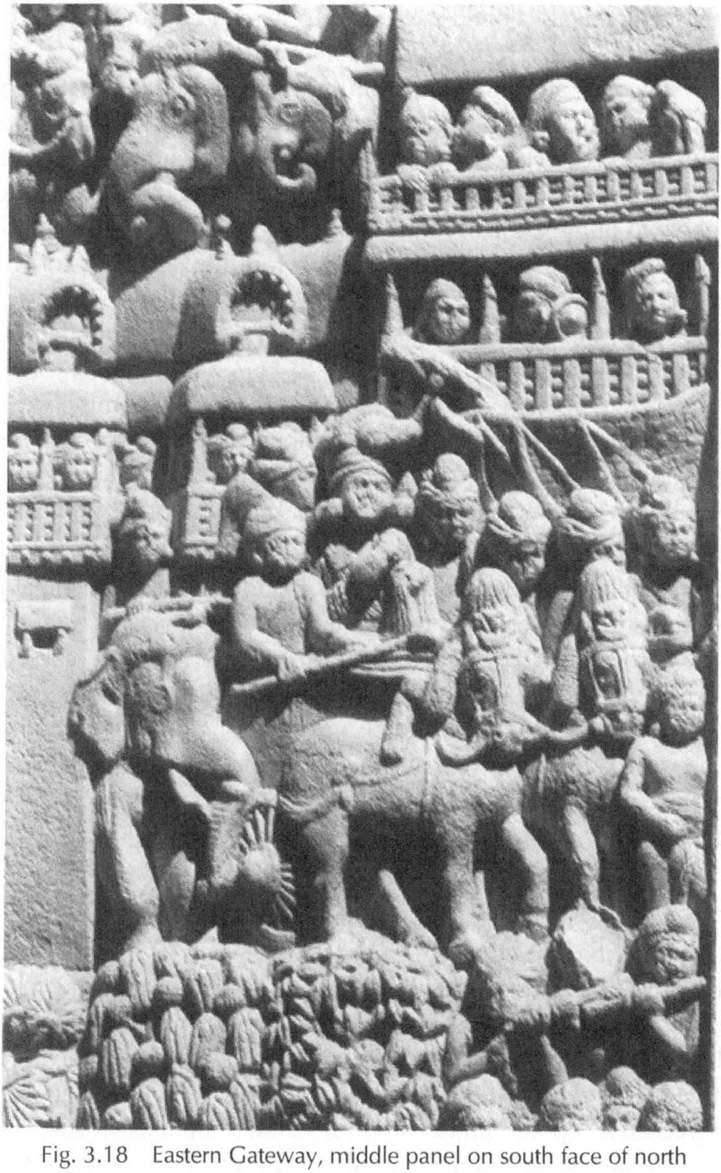

Fig. 3.18 Eastern Gateway, middle panel on south face of north pillar

3. The third panel from the top (Figs 3.17 and 3.18) contains three different events of one story. It depicts the story of Buddha's

visit to Kapilavastu. Buddha was earnestly requested by his father, Shuddhodana, to pay a visit to Kapilavastu as he had been away for seven years after his Mahabhinishkramana. Buddha therefore goes to Kapilavastu. Shuddhodana comes with his clansmen, the Shakyas, to receive him and meet his disciples who then stay in the banyan park presented by the king. Here Buddha performs a miracle to impress the Shakyas and walks in the air. They are all astonished and prostrate themselves before him. A noteworthy feature of this panel is the grouping of figures which look down diagonally from above. The depiction of the architectural details of storied mansions is interesting.

In the upper part of the panel, Shuddhodana is coming with the Shakyas to receive Buddha in Kapilavastu (Fig. 3.18). The narration continues in the middle part, and in the lower part we see a Bodhi tree and the astonished Shakyas looking up at where Buddha walked in the air.

4. In the panel at the bottom (Fig. 3.17) is a standing dvarapala identical to those on the other gateways.

On the squarish blocks between the architraves are carved the Nativity scene and the dharma-chakra on the left, and the Bodhi tree and the Nativity scene again on the right; the uprights in between the architraves have the Bodhi tree, the dharma-chakra on the lion pillar, and the lion pillar. There are, in addition, couples riding bulls and winged lions (Fig. 3.22)

Top architrave—front

1. *Manushi Buddhas (Fig. 3.19)*

The panel is entirely occupied by Manushi Buddhas represented by stupas and trees which are flanked by devout worshippers. The two trees are of Shakyamuni and Vipashyin respectively. At either end are animal (bull) riders and stupas. The central upright, between the top and middle architraves, has a pillar with a lion capital crowned by a dharma-chakra. The uprights on the sides have plants with jewelled necklaces. On the squarish blocks on the left is Maya seated on a lotus, being bathed by elephants,

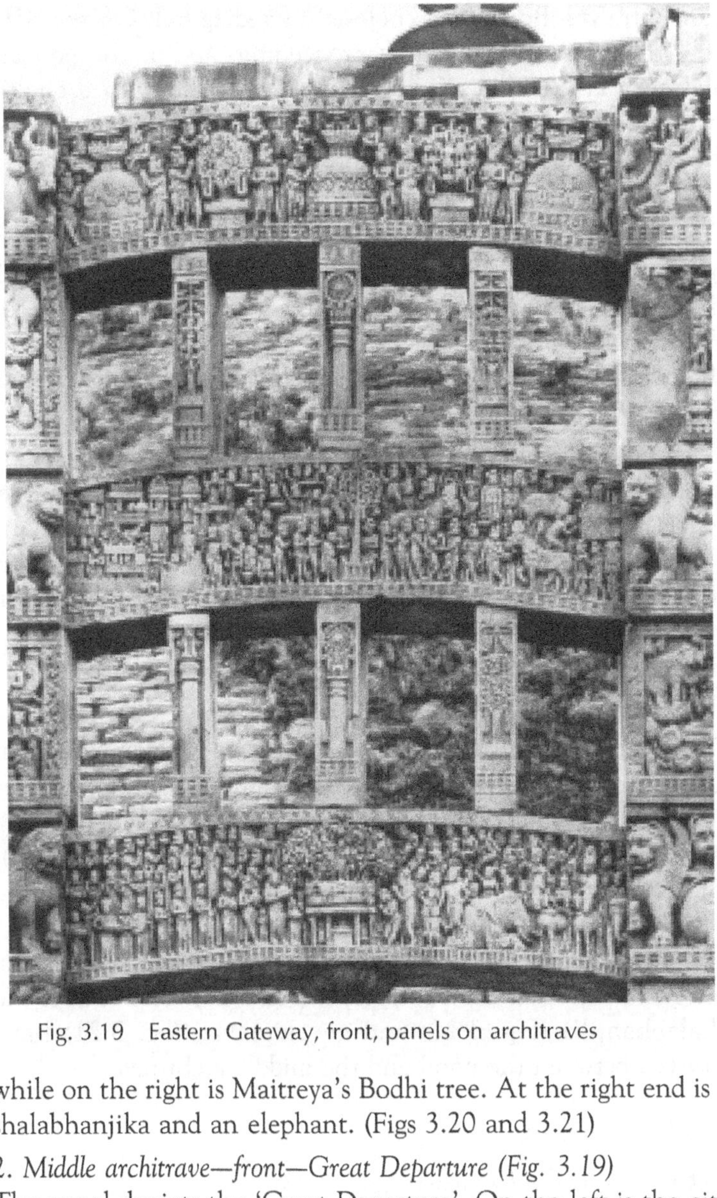

Fig. 3.19 Eastern Gateway, front, panels on architraves

while on the right is Maitreya's Bodhi tree. At the right end is a shalabhanjika and an elephant. (Figs 3.20 and 3.21)

2. *Middle architrave—front—Great Departure (Fig. 3.19)*

The panel depicts the 'Great Departure'. On the left is the city of Kapilavastu with storied houses and their inhabitants. A horse without a rider is coming out of the city gate with a retinue. In the centre is a Bodhi tree enclosed in vedica rail. On the right side, the horse (Kanthaka) is proceeding, and at the end are *Buddha-pada* (Buddha's feet) which are marked with a chakra (wheel), indicating that Buddha was a universal sovereign. At the ends of the architrave, on on either side, are elephants.

3. *First sermon and the Birth of Buddha*

The motifs on the uprights, between the middle and the lowest architraves, are similar to those above, and on the squarish block on the left is the 'Nativity' scene, while on the right is shown the 'First Sermon' of Buddha at Sarnath. Buddha is represented by a dharma-chakra on a throne with worshippers on either side. (Fig. 3.19).

4. *Lowest architrave—Ashoka's visit (Fig. 3.19)*

The scene on the right portrays Ashoka's visit to the Bodhi tree, which is in the centre, issuing out of a circular shrine. The king has come with his retinue, and elephants, horses, and members of the royal party crowd the panel. Queen Tishya-rakshita is on an elephant. On the left of the shrine are devotees.

Top architrave—back

The entire space is occupied by the seven Manushi Buddhas represented by their respective trees. From the right: (1) Fig tree (Shikhin), (2) Shala (Vishvabhu), (3) Shirisha (Krakuchchhanda), (4) Udumbara (Kanakamuni), (5) Nyagrodha (Kashyapa), (6) Ashvattha (Shakya muni), and (7) Patali of Vipashyin (Fig. 3.23).

The uprights are carved with palmettes and animal riders, and stupas, as usual, are also present (Fig. 3.22). The back of the Shalabhanjika (Fig. 3.20) and an elephant (Fig. 3.21) have survived between the pond and the middle architrave.

Middle architrave—back

Buddha worshipped by animals (Fig. 3.23)

According to a legend, Buddha once grew fed up of quarrels among the Shakyas, his clansmen, and therefore out of sheer disgust went to a forest for solitude where there were wild

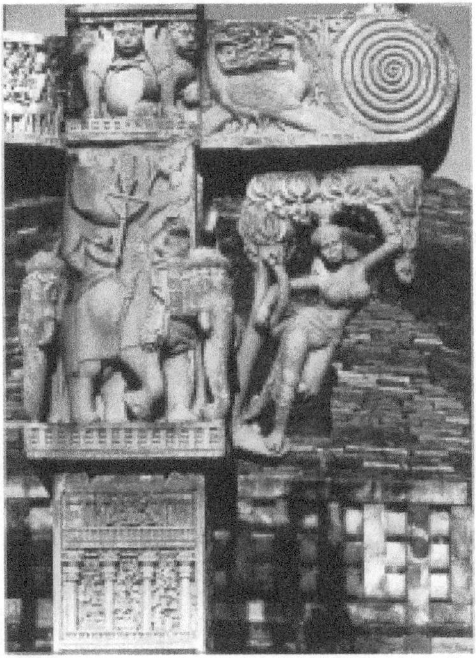

Fig. 3.20 Eastern Gateway, front, shalabhanjika

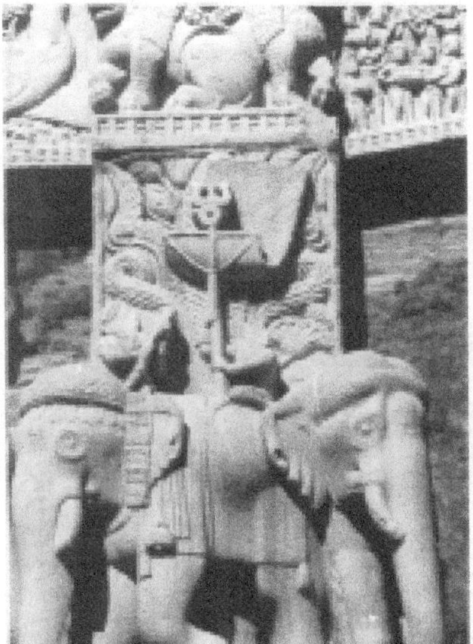

Fig. 3.21 Eastern Gateway, front, elephant capital

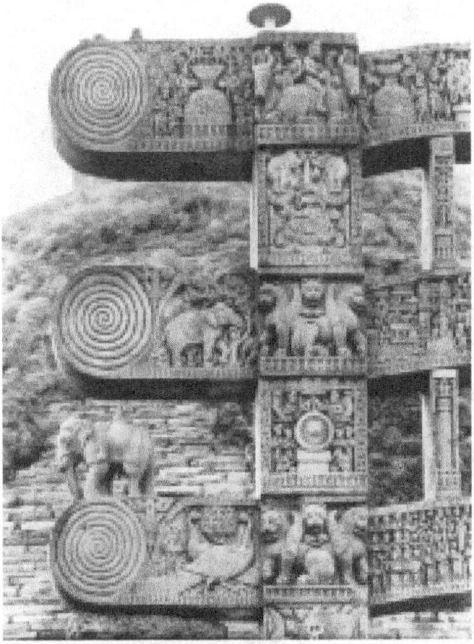

Fig. 3.22 Eastern Gateway, back, panels on architraves

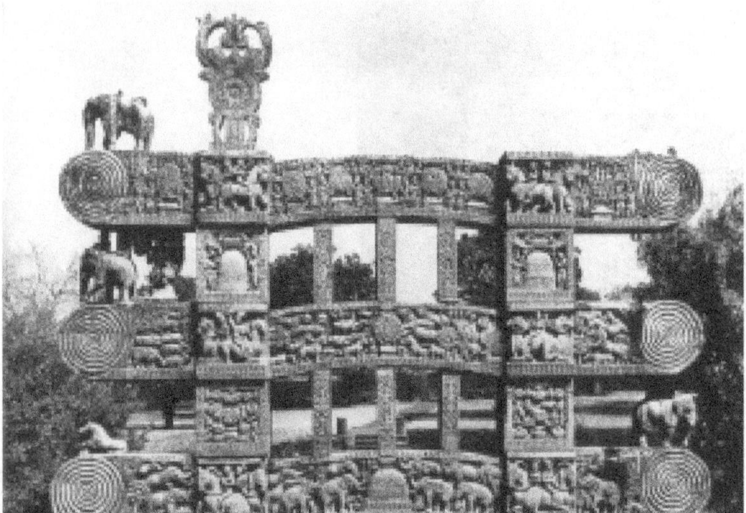

Fig. 3.23 Eastern Gateway, back, panels on architraves

elephants. In this panel, the artist has taken some liberty and has shown, with great imagination, a variety of animals including lions and tigers, and huge cobras adoring a Bodhi tree in the centre. It is also likely that the *Sama Jataka* is portrayed here. The *Jataka* tells us that Buddha was born in one of his previous lives as Sama, a young anchorite, and was living in the forest in the company of wild animals. In the *Chariya Pitaka*, a Buddhist text, Buddha himself recounts that when he was the young Sama, he lived in the forest in the company of lions, tigers, bears, and other animals. This is what we see in the panel.

On the side blocks there are camel riders, and the uprights are similar to those above.

Lowest architrave—back (Fig. 3.23)

The entire lowest architrave is carved with a stupa in the centre which is being worshipped by elephants. On the squarish blocks are animal riders; the animals look like goats or antelopes.

Northern Gateway (Fig. 3.24)

Of the four gateways, the finest and the most complete is the Northern Gateway. It was found standing *in situ* and did not need any reconstruction, as was the case with the other gateways. It gives a fair idea as to how the gateways must have looked when they were standing in their pristine glory. The Northern Gateway is the best preserved, with most of its decorative ornamentation intact. Its pillar capitals have elephants—rather their foreparts—which are richly ornamented with large bead strings and bells. Most noteworthy are the large jewelled bands around the heads, with auspicious symbols as pendants. The elephants have female mahouts and in between them are palmettes.

All the gateways were lavishly decorated with elegant carvings and even sculptures in the round, but it is only the Northern Gateway which, being still *in situ*, has retained most of them. Besides the reliefs on architraves and pillars, the spaces in between have also been embellished with sculptures in the round so that they can be seen from both sides. This space is divided by means

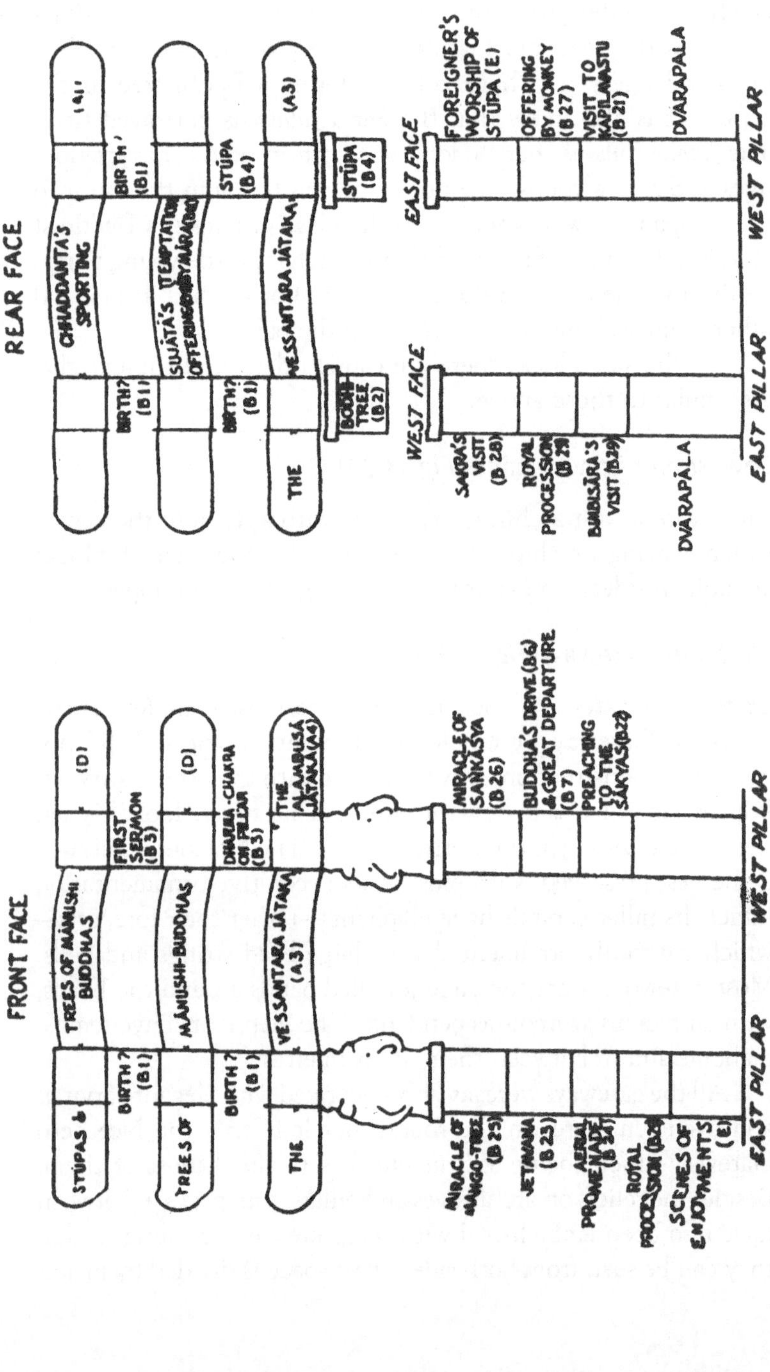

Fig. 3.24 Northern Gateway, location of panels

of uprights which are also are carved on both faces. They are ornamented with horse riders in the upper row and elephant riders (couples) in the lower, while on the volutes are seated lions.

The most remarkable, however, are the shalabhanjikas—the beautiful damsels standing by or clinging to a tree (Fig. 3.25). This is a common motif in Indian art even in the later period. Convention has it that an Ashoka tree flowers when kicked by a beautiful damsel. They are also referred to as *vrikshikas* and are shown in most alluring postures, usually flexed, wearing heavy jewellery and complex headdresses. With nestling breasts and swaying hips, they appear most sensuous. What is more, they wear a diaphanous lower garment (*antariya*) which reveals even the private parts. They are celestial nymphs. Their supple form and telling grace is very artistically delineated. They are not heavy, earth bound *yakshis* like those at Bharhut, but have shed their weight which has lent them an easy repose. They are carved in the round and constitute true sculpture which is rare in Indian art in which much of the sculpture forms part of architecture. Their facial beauty is remarkable, but their nudity is enigmatic, especially in the Buddhist context. This may, in all probability, be due to the motifs derived from the ancient fertility cults which influenced the early art of Buddhists as well as that of Jains and Hindus.

The Northern Gateway is thus a very imposing torana which is crowned by a huge dharma-chakra (Wheel of Law), in the centre of the uppermost architrave. It was flanked by a huge attendant yaksha on either side, beyond which are tri-ratnas, and at the end, over the volute ends, are lions facing opposite directions. Some of these motifs, however, have vanished; the dharma-chakra is broken, as is the tri-ratna on the left, while the yaksha on the left is totally missing.

On the squarish blocks, slightly projecting between the architraves, we see the Nativity scene in which mother Maya is shown standing on a lotus, being bathed by elephants; there are dharma-chakras (Wheels of Law) and animal riders in between.

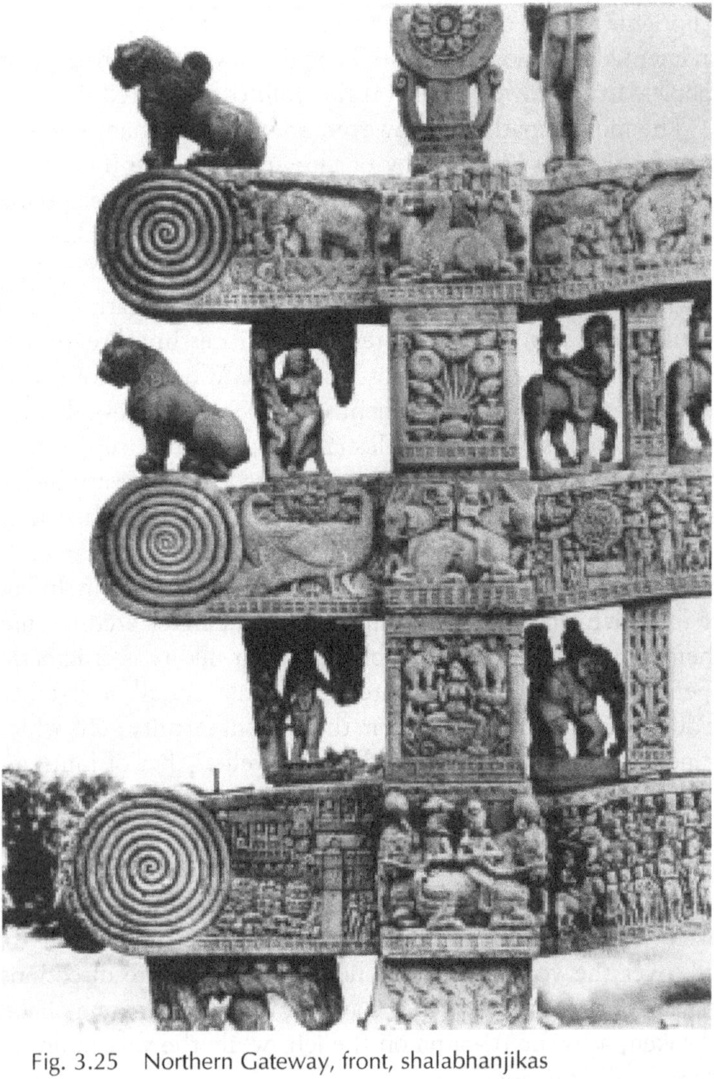

Fig. 3.25 Northern Gateway, front, shalabhanjikas

In between the pillars and the architraves are four elephants with their bodies merged; they have a rider each and by their side is a voluptuous shalabhanjika (Fig. 3.25).

East pillar—front face

1. *Top—Miracle of the Mango Tree* (Fig. 3.26)

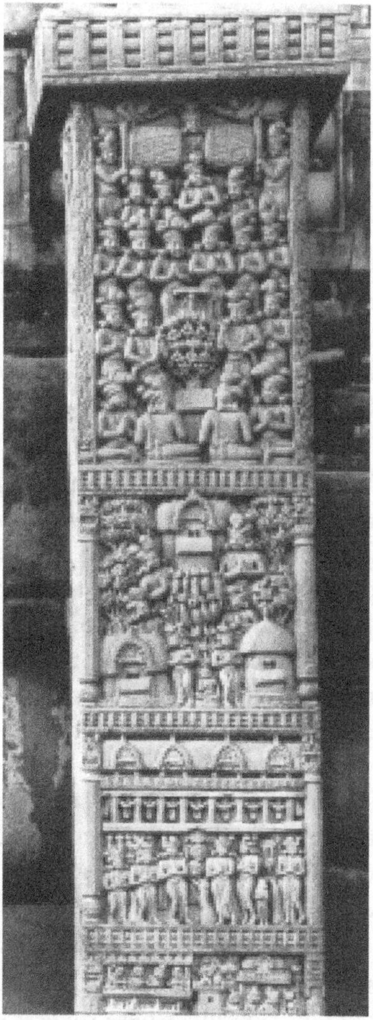

Fig. 3.26 Northern Gateway, east pillar, front face

This story is a part of the legend 'Miracle of Sravasti' which Buddha had performed. He had to do it to confound six heretical teachers. He performed a number of feats in the presence of king Prasenjit and one of these was the 'Miracle of the Mango Tree', in which Buddha caused a mango tree to grow. In the panel, there is a mango tree laden with fruit. According to Buddhist texts, it was under a mango tree that Buddha performed a great miracle at Sravasti by walking in mid-air when flames issued out of his feet and water flowed from his head. In the panel, an empty throne symbolizing Buddha is shown below the mango tree. There are four men in front of it, one of whom must be Prasenjit, the king of Kosala. The personages in the upper part are in all likelihood gods. At the top are two big drums—a sort of war drum (*dundubhi*)—which are being beaten by a man with a club, and above are flying *gandharvas* hovering in the sky.

2. *Jetavana* (Fig. 3.26)

The next panel is carved with the story of Anathapindaka. He was a wealthy merchant of Sravasti who became an ardent devotee of Buddha and was converted to Buddhism. He built a great monastery for Buddha for which he purchased land from prince Jeta, paying as many gold coins as would cover the entire land. The coins can be seen as square pieces on the ground at the bottom of the panel. The most prominent figure on the right is probably the merchant Anathapindaka who purchased the park (Jetavana), and the one on the left may be prince Jeta. The three buildings are Buddha's favourite residences, the Gandha-kuti, Kosamba-kuti, and Karori-kuti.

3. *Aerial promenade* (Fig. 3.26)

We see in this panel an imposing building, with a wagon-vaulted roof decorated with chaitya arches in front. Inside, some people are standing in adoration. Above them is a broad band which probably represents the aerial path (*chankama*) where Buddha walked. This identification is based on the evidence of a similar, but more convincing, representation at Bharhut, without which the identification of this panel would have been difficult. Since Buddha could not be shown in human form, the problem naturally was how to illustrate the event. The artist has very ingeniously shown people facing upwards, suggesting that they are watching the miracle. But then the question that arises is: have the people understood the significance?

4. *Royal Procession* (Fig. 3.27)

There are quite a few panels showing royal personages visiting a stupa. It is not, however, possible to identify them all, as can be done at Bharhut where there are label inscriptions. The present scene may represent the visit of Prasenjit, who was the king of Kosala. He is shown passing through a city gate of Sravasti, his capital, with his retinue; in the upper part are storied houses from which people are watching the procession.

5. *Lowest panel* (Fig. 3.27)

There are a few scenes which portray the day-to-day life of common people, doing their daily chores, and enjoying the small

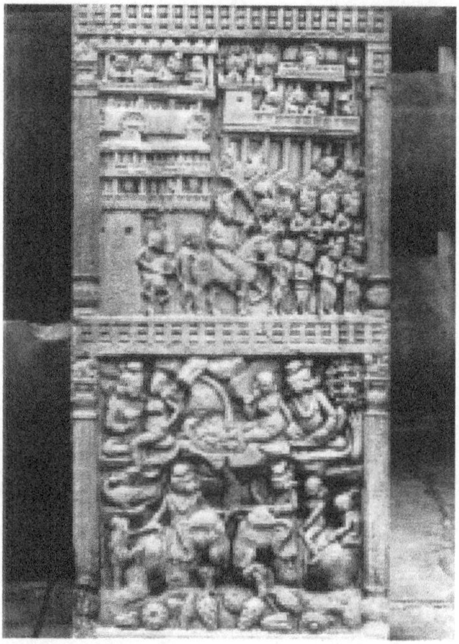

Fig. 3.27 Northern Gateway, east pillar, front face

pleasures of life. The present scene is one such in which contemporary life is reflected. The Buddhist art of Sanchi thus constitutes a documentary on the life of the people in India in the 1st century BC. In the upper part of the panel is a couple drinking and another frolicking, further down are royal personages on elephants, and in the forefront is a lotus pond.

East pillar—west face

1. The upper panel on the inner face of the east pillar depicts Indra's visit (Fig. 3.28). Shakra, accompanied by his musician Panchashikha, is said to have visited Buddha at his Indra-shaila cave near Rajagriha. In the upper part of the panel is the rock-cut cave with a stupa (or seat?), and below this are a number of votaries standing in adoration.

2. In the central part (Fig. 3.29) we see a procession showing a royal personage leaving through the city gate, and citizens watching from the balconies of their storied mansions.

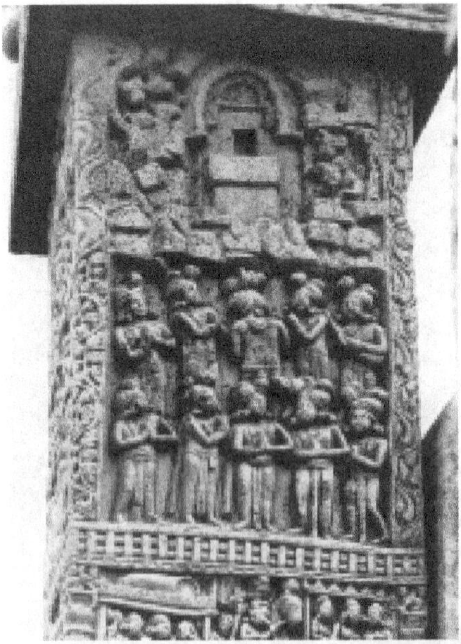

Fig. 3.28 Northern Gateway, east pillar, west face

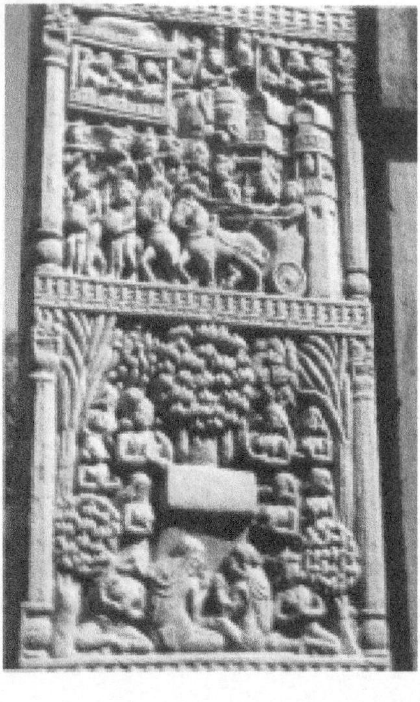

Fig. 3.29 Northern Gateway, east pillar, west face

3. In the lowest panel is the Bodhi tree surrounded by worshippers seated with folded hands.

4. The guardian (dvarapala) is a robust, young man, wearing a *dhoti* (*antariya*) as his lower garment which is tied round the waist with the front pleats left dangling between the legs; they resemble the trunk of an elephant and hence have been referred to in literature as the *hasti-shundaka* fashion. He also wears an *uttariya* (upper garment), the tuft of which is seen on the right. His hair is combed into a ball which, at the front, is secured in a turban. He wears elaborate jewellery, heavy ear pendants, beaded bracelets, and a broad necklace composed of several strings which are passed through two spacers and hence can be identified as of the *dviphalaka* variety. His flexed position shows his alertness.

There is a similar guardian on the east face of the west pillar, though it is partly broken.

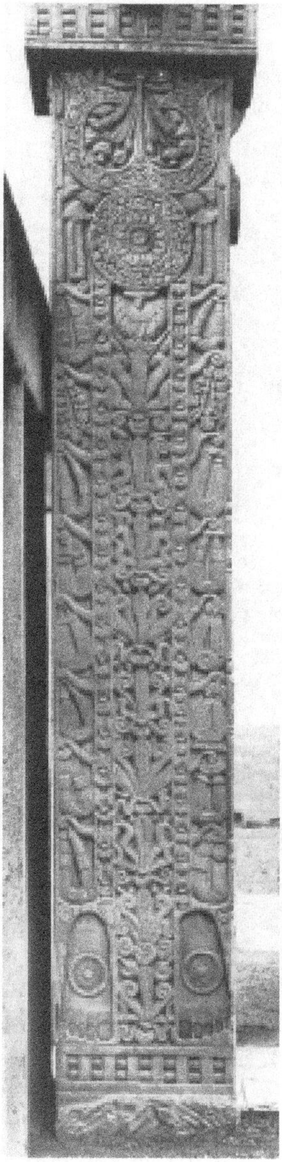

Fig. 3.30 Northern Gateway, east pillar, east face and west pillar, west face

East pillar—east face and west pillar—west face (Fig. 3.30)

It is a richly carved pattern consisting of a central band filled with palmettes, one above the other, that looks almost like a creeper. It is common to both the pillars and the only difference is that the west pillar has the same pattern repeated on the side bands, whereas

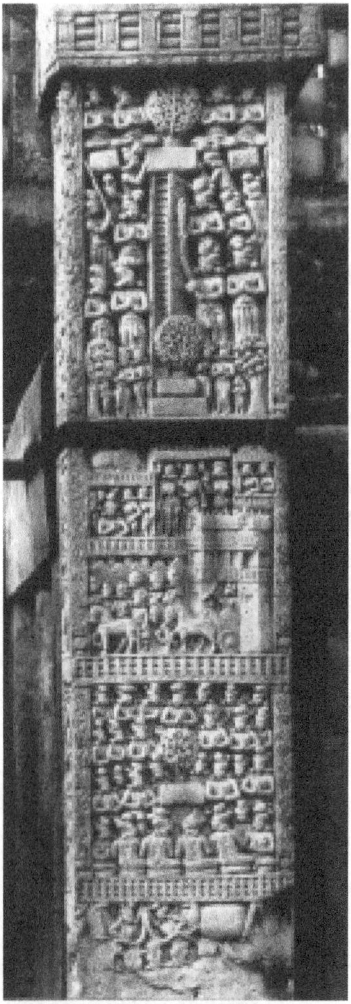

Fig. 3.31 Northern Gateway, west pillar, front face

the east pillar has Buddha-pada (Buddha's feet) at the base and a beautiful tri-ratna at the top. On the side bands are jewelled necklaces hanging from pegs. Among these there are two varieties, one consisting of thirteen and the other of eleven amulets. They are: *Sun*, *Shukra*, *padmasara*, *ankusha* (elephant goad), *Vaijayanti*, *pankaja* (lotus), *mina-mithuna* (two fish), *srivatsa*, *parashu* (battle axe), *darpana* (mirror), and *kamala* (lotus). These were supposed to be auspicious symbols. Later in the Kushan period, the number is reduced to eight and they are then referred to as ashta-mangalaka *haras*. The necklaces are suspended from pegs that look like elephant tusks (*naga-danta*).

The inscription on the east pillar reads: "*Bhagavato pamana lathi*," meaning 'Buddha's measuring rod.'

West pillar—front face

1. *Top—The Miracle of Sankasya* (Fig. 3.31)

In the middle of the panel is a ladder or a flight of steps with a Bodhi tree at the bottom as well as at the top, and there are a number of people, including couples, on either side. The panel can be identified as the 'Miracle of Sankasya' in which Buddha, after performing the 'Miracle of Sravasti', vanished and went to the Tryastrimsha heaven to preach *abhidharma* (Law) to his mother who was reborn there. He stayed there for three months, and descended by a staircase of beryl at Sankasya along with Shakra (Indra) and Brahma. They are both shown prominently in the middle of the panel.

2. *Buddha's four drives and the Great Departure* (Fig. 3.31)
The middle pannel is carved with two events of Buddha's life. (i) The four drives of Buddha: In the course of his drives through Kapilavastu, Gautam saw an old man, a sick man, a corpse, and an ascetic. In the panel he is shown going in a chariot out of the city gate, but he is not seen in it. (ii) Next to this is a horse without a rider (that is, Buddha) which marks his 'Great Departure' from the palace after giving up a luxurious life.

3. *Preaching to the Shakyas* (Fig. 3.31)
In the centre of the panel is a tree around which a number of persons are sitting in adoration. The panel depicts Buddha (represented by the tree) preaching to the Shakyas, his own clansmen, in the *Nyagrodha-arama* in Kapilavastu.

4. There was one more panel (Fig. 3.31) below but this is now destroyed. What we see is a large kettle drum (dundubhi) and flying kinnaras, which may be a part of the 'Miracle of Sravasti'.

West pillar—east face (Fig. 3.32)

1. The upper part of the panel depicts a stupa within an enclosure with a gateway like that at Sanchi itself. It is flanked by kinnaras with bodies of birds, and below them are votaries with hands folded in adoration. In the lower part are two rows of men rejoicing on the occasion and adoring the stupa. Most of them are musicians playing on musical instruments such as drums: one is of the *ankya* type which is horizontal and is held in the lap, and the other is of the *urdhvaka* variety which is placed vertically. One person is playing upon a gourd shaped lute (*vina*), and the others are blowing long, curved trumpets, the ends of which look like cobra heads. But a very curious instrument, which is rare in India, is the double flute or the Pan pipe which is of Greek origin. Equally interesting is the dress of the musicians. They wear knee-length skirts

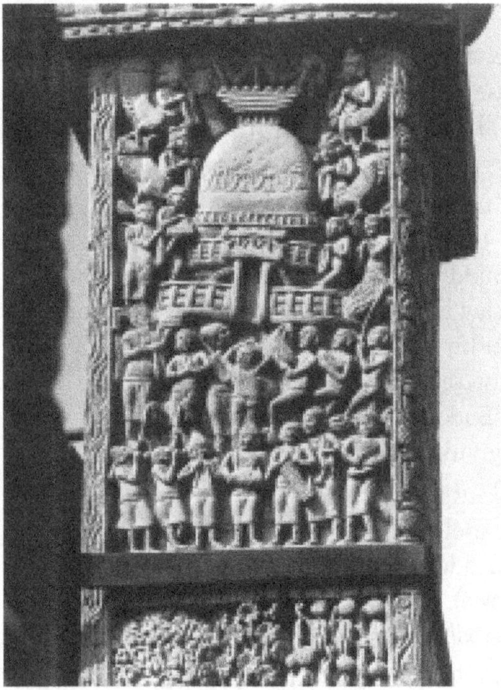

Fig. 3.32 Northern Gateway, west pillar, east face

(*chandataka*), half sleeved tunics (*kurpasaka*), and flowing cloaks (*achchhadanaka*) secured at the front in a clasp. Their conical caps and sandals with leggings clearly indicate that they are foreigners. They can be identified as the Shakas (Scythians) of the Tigrakhauda clan who wore pointed headgear. Their presence in a Buddhist shrine may appear enigmatic, but it must be borne in mind that Buddhism had spread beyond the Indian frontiers and the Shakas had started coming to India from the north-west. Many of them became Buddhists and this explains their presence in Indian art. The panel in question is undoubtedly the work of an experienced artist as the figures are full of life.

2. On the left (Fig. 3.33) is a huge Bodhi tree and monkeys are shown bringing offerings; there are other people also. This is the representation of one of the eight important events in Buddha's life. When he was at Vaishali, a monkey is said to have brought honey to him, according to a touching story.

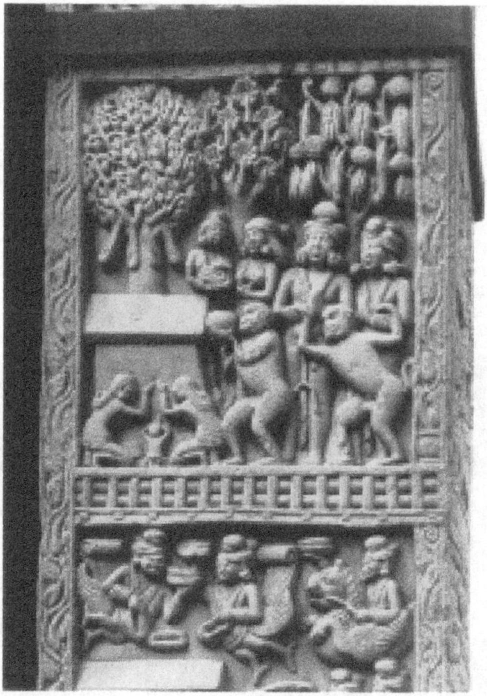

Fig. 3.33 Northern Gateway, west pillar, east face

3. When Buddha returned to Kapilavastu after gaining 'Enlightenment', his father Shuddhodana came along with his retinue to receive him. But the problem was who should honour whom first, because although Shuddhodana was the king and father, Gautam had become Buddha. The latter saved the situation by performing a miracle: he walked in the air. The story is partly depicted on the east face of the west pillar where, in front of a banyan tree, is an empty throne symbolizing Buddha, and in the air is shown the promenade (chankama) where Buddha is supposed to have walked. There are flying kinnaras with garlands in their hands. Shuddhodana, with his retinue and an umbrella over his head, is standing to the right of the tree. The banyan tree (*Ficus indica*, Sk. nyagrodha) symbolizes the park of banyan trees which Shuddhodana gifted to his son, Buddha.

Front face—top architrave

1. *Trees of Manushi Buddhas* (Fig. 3.34)

This is the representation of Manushi Buddhas which also occurs on the other gateways. Here we see only five, three stupas and two Bodhi trees. They occupy the entire lintel. They are the

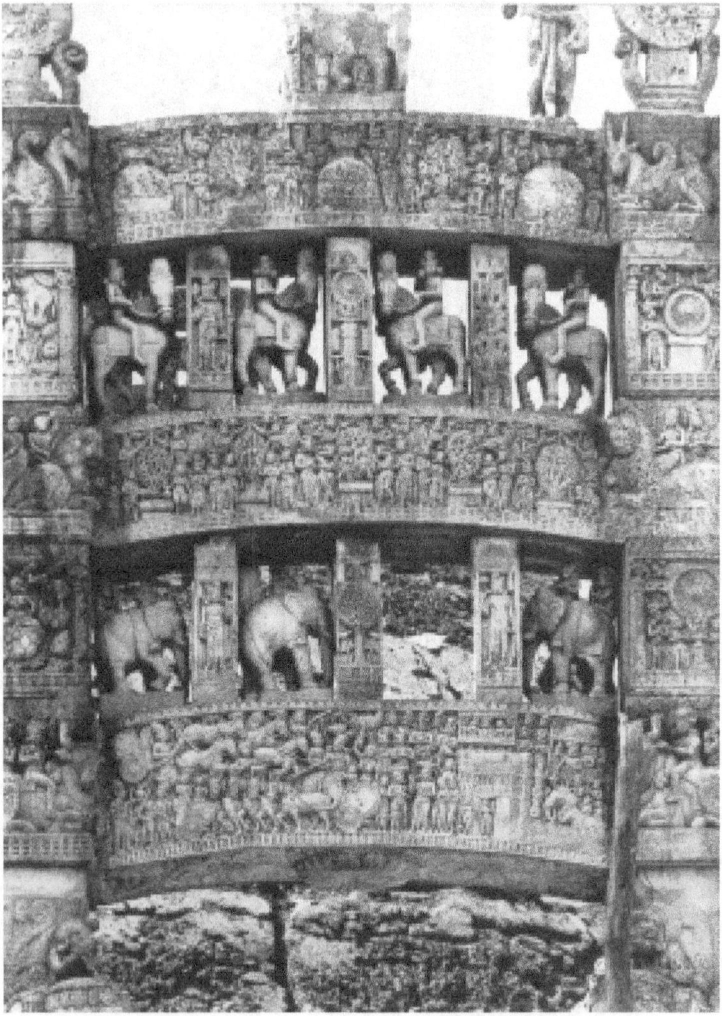

Fig. 3.34 Northern Gateway, front, panels on architraves

ashvattha (*Ficus religiosa*) and nyagrodha (*Ficus indica*) of Shakyamuni and Kashyapa respectively.

2. *The middle architrave* (Fig. 3.34)

This is also completely occupied by Manushi Buddhas and all the seven are present. They are, from the left: (1) Patali or *Bignonia* of Vipashyin; (2) fig tree of Shikhin; (3) Shala of Vishvabhu; (4) Shirisha of Krakuchchhanda; (5) Udumbara of Kanakamuni; (6) Nyagrodha of Kashyapa; and (7) Ashvattha of Shakyamuni. A similar panel at Bharhut has label inscriptions which have helped identification.

3. *Lowest architrave—Vessantara Jataka* (Fig. 3.34)

This *Jataka* story was also a favourite of the ancient Indian artist. In this, Bodhisattva was born as prince Vessantara (sk. Vishvantara), who was known for his charity and compassion. His father, king Sanjaya, was forced by his subjects to banish him from the Sibi kingdom to Mount Vanka as punishment, because he had given away an elephant endowed with supernatural powers of causing rain to the brahmins of Kalinga, which was suffering from drought. The prince had, therefore, to leave the city in a chariot along with his wife Maddi and his son and daughter. On the way, he gave away first the horses and then the chariot to the people who asked for them. He then reached Mount Vanka on foot, and lived there with his family in a hermitage which was provided to him by the god Shakra (Indra). Later he gifted away his children to Jujuka, a brahmin, and even his wife to Shakra, who came to him in the disguise of a brahmin. But Shakra gave her back to him and, through his grace, also reunited Vessantara with his father who in turn, freed the children by paying ransom to Jujuka. The story brings out the boundless charity of prince Vessantara. It has been carved with a wealth of detail on the front and back of the lowest architrave of the Northern Gateway. The continuous narration of different events is noteworthy as it helps in understanding the story, as is the case with the *Chhadanta Jataka* depicted on the Southern Gateway.

4. *Lowest architrave—front and back*

The story of prince Vessantara continues from the right end of the middle section of the lowest architrave. Below is depicted the rampart of the royal capital with battlements, above which is the prince riding the elephant which he gifted to the drought-stricken people of Kalinga. He is then banished and is seen outside the city gate in a four-horse chariot along with his family, and is taking leave of the people. Later, the chariot is also given away. On the left, near the voluted end, stands Vessantara, his wife Maddi with a child on her hip, and people with folded hands. Above this is the hermitage which Shakra had built for the prince to live in during his exile. There are villagers holding bows and arrows, and others returning from the forest with hunted deer on their shoulders. There is also a lion who has detained Maddi. This is depicted on the back of the architrave.

Front face—right end of lowest architrave—Ambulasha Jataka

The panel depicts the *Ambulasha Jataka* in which Buddha (Bodhisattva) was born as an ascetic with whom a doe fell in love. In course of time she gave birth to a male child who was like a normal human being except for a single horn on his head which he had inherited from his mother. He was therefore named Isisinga (Rishyashringa or Ekashringa). Like his father, he also became an ascetic. His greatness and power became a threat to Shakra's (Indra) position as the king of gods. He therefore deputed Ambulasha, a nymph, to lure Rishyashringa. She was successful in her task but did not reveal the main purpose of her mission. She kept it a closely guarded secret for three years but later revealed it. Rishyashringa, being a great ascetic and full of compassion, forgave her and sent her back to heaven. In the panel, the entire story is crowded for want of space. The ascetic is shown seated in front of his leaf-covered hut (parna-kuti) and a doe is seen lying at his feet. At the back she is shown giving birth to a child with one horn on his head—like a sort of unicorn. He is taking a bath in a lotus pond. On the left he is standing before his father, the ascetic.

Top Architrave—back (Fig. 3.35)

The entire space on this architrave has been occupied by the *Chhadanta Jataka*, the story of the six-tusked elephant, but there are not as many details as on the back of the Southern Gateway.

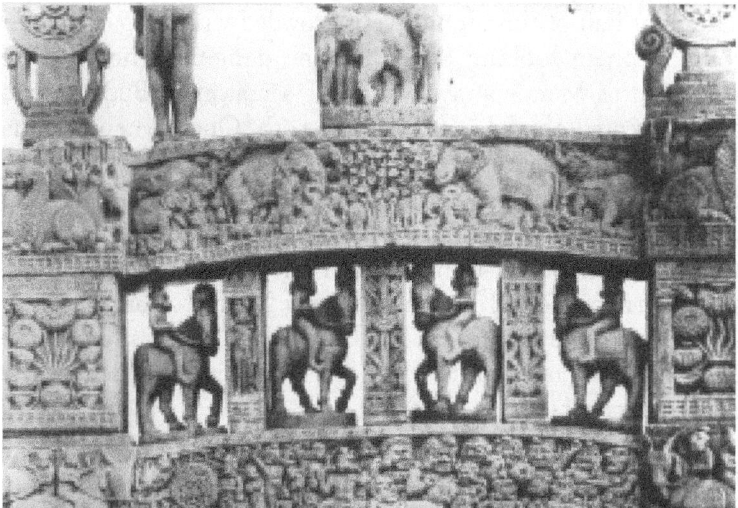

Fig. 3.35 Northern Gateway, back, panels on architraves

The dharma-chakra and the tri-ratnas which were seen on the front part of the gateway, are also carved on the back, as are the shalabhanjikas. In the Nativity scene carved on a squarish block, Maya is shown seated with elephants bathing her. On the corresponding panel is a stupa with worshippers.

Middle architrave—back

Sujata offering food/Mara's temptation (Fig. 3.35)
The right half of this architrave is crowded with human figures, some of them looking like gruesome demons. They can be identified as Mara's army. Mara was a cousin of Buddha who always created obstacles in Buddha's path. Once, when Buddha was meditating, he sent his six beautiful daughters to distract him, but was unsuccessful. He then sent his army of demons. On the left, Buddha is represented by the Bodhi tree. The female with a tray is Sujata bringing food for Buddha. Next is Mara seated on a throne and directing his army. Mara's son and daughter are shown to the right of the Bodhi tree. The composition of the panel is indeed noteworthy for in the crowd one can identify the major characters.

Lowest architrave—back (Fig. 3.35)

The *Vessantara Jataka* is continued here on the front and four events can be identified: (1) life in the hermitage, (2) the gift of the children, (3) the gift of the wife, and (4) the final reunion. Parts of the story are also found on the back of the Northern Gateway at the eastern and western ends, which shows the importance of the panel.

Top—back

At the top of the gateway, at the back, is a huge tri-ratna with a yaksha attendant by its side, while in the centre was a dharma-chakra which is now completely broken, except for the supporting elephants at the base. (Fig. 3.36)

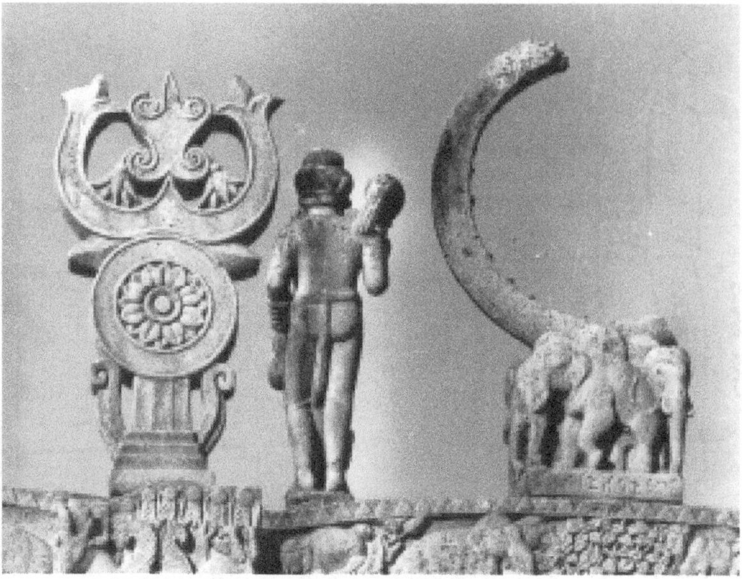

Fig. 3.36 Northern Gateway, top, back

Western Gateway (Figures 3.37 and 3.38)

This gateway has lost many of its features. All the carved uprights which are usually seen between architraves are missing, and the motifs crowning the top are also gone. Artistically, it is rather inferior to the other three gateways.

The pillar capitals have four corpulent yaksha-like figures (*kichakas*), standing back-to-back; their upraised hands support the architraves (Fig. 3.39). They are pot-bellied and have grotesque features. They wear sparse jewellery—only a necklace and thick bracelets—a short dhoti (*ardhoruka*) ending above the knees, and a turban from which the ball of hair protrudes at the front.

North pillar—front (Fig. 3.40)

Two panels have been carved on the front face of the pillar of which the lower is almost fully destroyed, save in the upper margin. The upper panel is divided into four scenes in two rows of two each, separated by a vedica rail. They illustrate couples (*mithunas*)

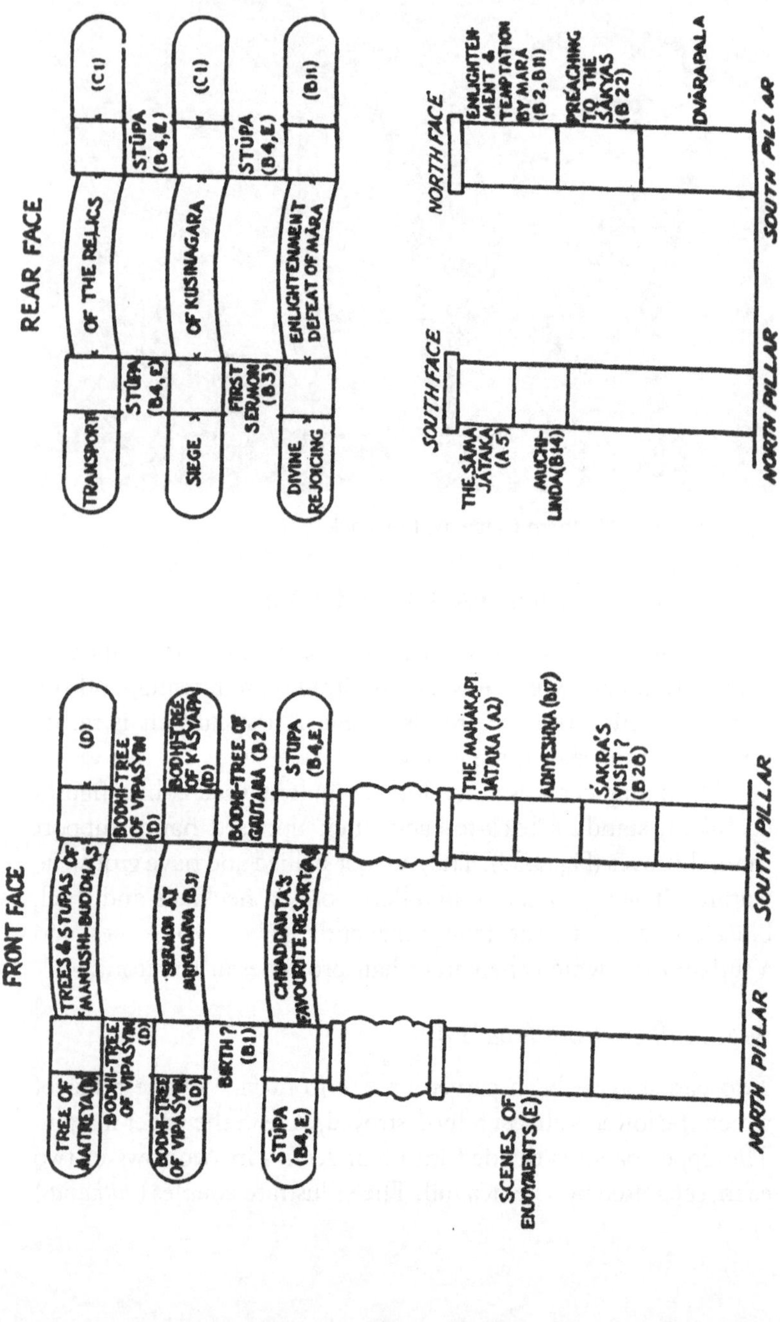

Fig. 3.37 Western Gateway, location of panels

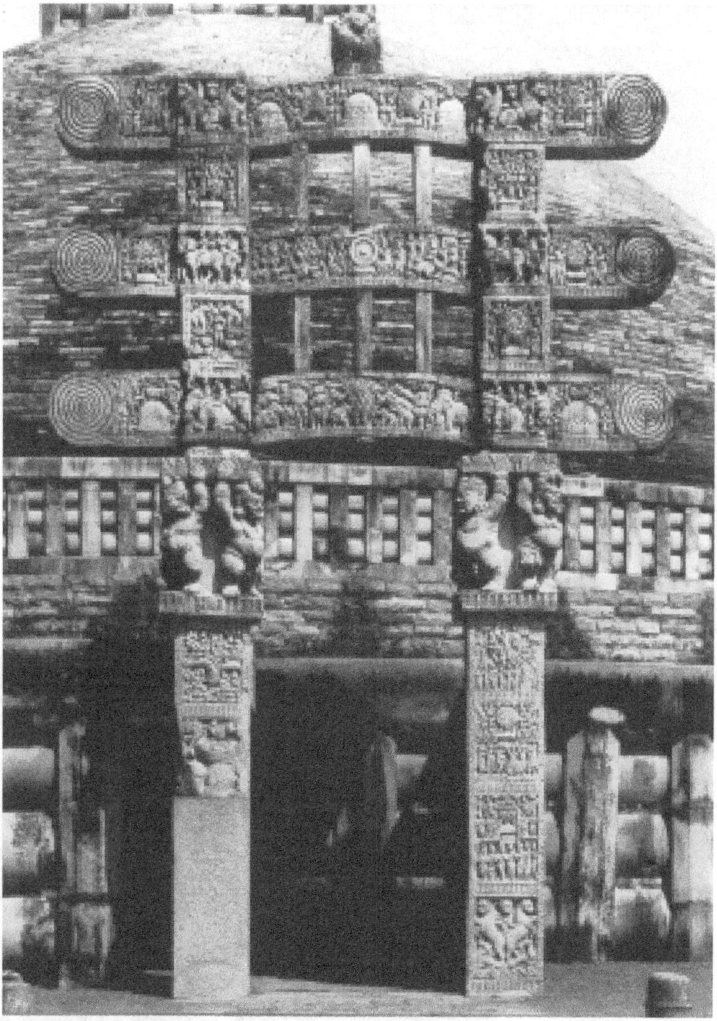

Fig. 3.38 Western Gateway, front

enjoying the pleasures of life. They seem to be sitting on couches under a tree in a garden. In the upper row is one more couple in the middle: they are shown standing on steps and are in a very intimate posture. The panel on the left at the top shows a woman engaged in toilet as she has a mirror in her left hand; her consort

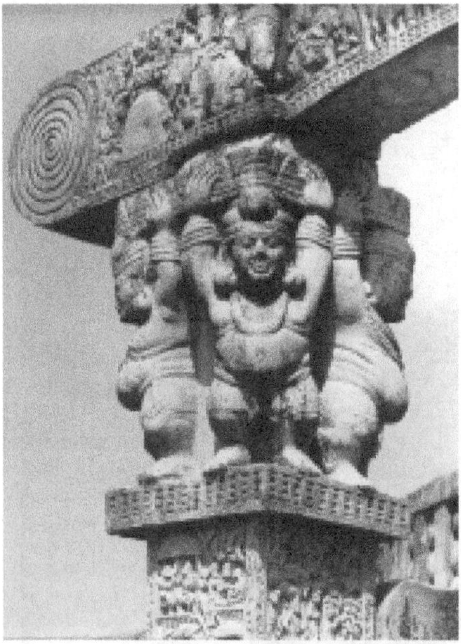

Fig. 3.39 Western Gateway, front, pillar capital

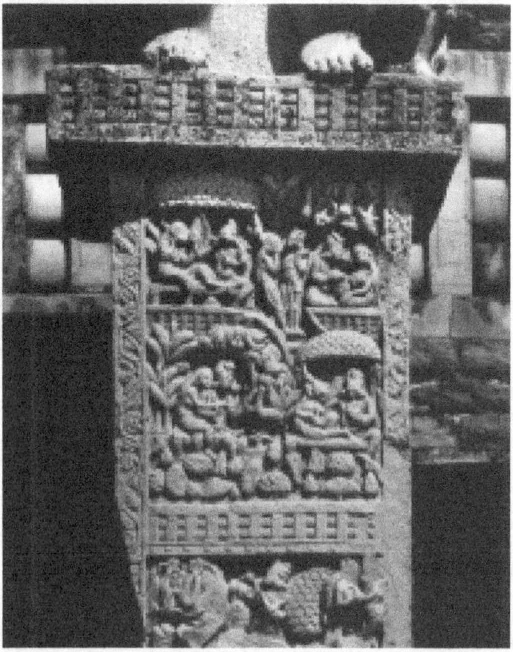

Fig. 3.40 Western Gateway, north pillar, front

is taking out jewellery from the tree which seems to be a kalpa-vriksha (wish-fulfilling tree). The couple on the upper right are talking intimately. The couples in the lower panels also seem to be engaged in conversation. That they are in a garden is clear from the lotus pond in front of them and the trees.

There were possibly similar scenes in the lower panel too, for in the left corner is the kalpa-vriksha from the branches of which jewellery hangs, on the right is a couple, and in the middle is a musician playing on a bow-shaped vina while his consort dances.

North pillar—south face

1. *Sama Jataka* (Fig. 3.41)

While many of the themes are repeated, this one occurs only once. Bodhisattva, born as Sama (Suvannasama), was devoted to his parents who had become blind because of a snake-bite. One day he went to the river to fetch water, but was shot with an arrow by the king of Varanasi. The arrow was poisonous and killed Sama. When the king came to know about the plight of his blind parents, he was full of remorse, and offered his services to them. However, by the grace of a goddess, Sama recovered his life and the parents their sight.

In the panel, at the top we see two huts in which Bodhisattva's parents are shown seated. Below, on the left, is the king as hunter with a bow and arrow. In front is the river or pond with lotuses, on the bank is Sama with a pitcher, and with him is probably Shakra (Indra). Deer and buffaloes indicate that it is a forest near a village.

2. *Naga Muchalinda* (Fig. 3.41)

Buddha is said to have spent the fifth week after gaining Enlightenment under a goatherd's nyagrodha tree and later went to Muchalinda where he was protected in a storm by the Naga king Muchalinda. In the upper part of the panel, we see the Bodhi tree with an umbrella (chhatra) over it, surrounded by worshippers. Below it, in the centre, is the Naga king Muchalinda with his retinue. There are also musicians in the group.

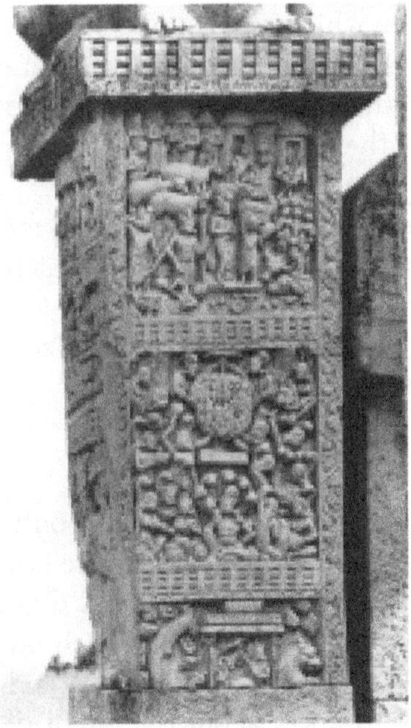

Fig. 3.41 Western Gateway, north pillar, south face

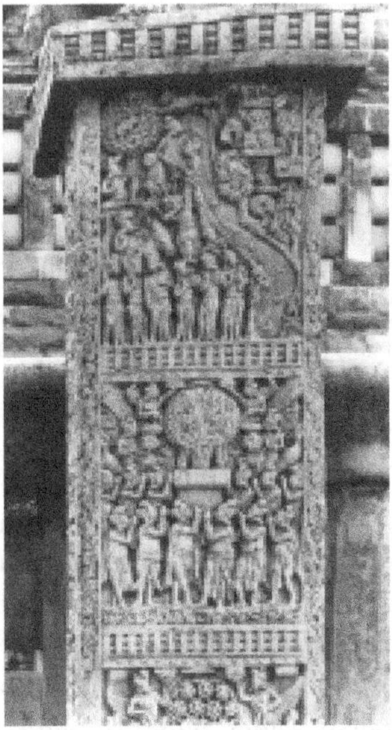

Fig. 3.42 Western Gateway, south pillar, front

3. The panel (Fig. 3.41) shows a royal couple in a boat which has a *vyala*-shaped prow and a stern resembling a fish tale. The water is indicated by wavy lines, and lotus flowers and creepers are seen in it.

South pillar—front

1. *Mahakapi Jataka* (Fig. 3.42)

This is a very interesting *Jataka* story according to which Buddha was born as a monkey in one of his previous lives. He was the leader of eighty thousand monkeys and lived with them in a mango grove on the banks of the Ganga in the Himalayas. The king of Varanasi, Brahmadatta, came to know about the delicious mangoes, and sent his soldiers to surround the grove. Bodhisattva jumped to the other bank and tied a bamboo to his waist to serve as a bridge. But that was not enough and he therefore spread his body to span the distance so that the monkeys could cross. His rival, Devadatta, who was also born as a monkey, jumped on him with great force, and as a result Bodhisattva's heart broke. The king was moved by this act, and brought him down. He then delivered a sermon to the king.

The panel shows the river, and at the top is the monkey forming a bridge by stretching his body. Then he is seen with the king under a tree. Down below is the king's retinue consisting of soldiers and musicians.

2. *Adhyeshana* (Fig. 3.42)
The scene is similar to that on the Eastern Gateway in which Buddha, represented by the Bodhi tree, is preaching to the gods who are shown in the lower part. There are kinnaras flanking the Bodhi tree.

3. *Shakra's visit*
The panel shows Indra's visit to Buddha, who is represented by the Bodhi tree in a cave. However, this is not as clear as on the Northern Gateway.

4. Three lions, one in the centre and two on the sides facing opposite directions, can be seen on this panel.

South pillar—north face

1. *Enlightenment and the Temptation of Mara* (Fig. 3.43)
The Bodhi tree in the upper part as usual symbolises Enlightenment; it has votaries around it. Below in the left hand corner is probably the Nairanjana river with lotuses, while on the right is the empty throne of Buddha. Among the figures, the central one is probably Mara who is trying to tempt Buddha. A noteworthy feature of this panel is that the artist has attempted to create an illusion of perspective by grading figures in two different planes, and diminishing the size of the figures in the upper plane so that they appear more distant.

2. *Preaching to the Shakyas* (Fig. 3.43)
Again, the Bodhi tree in the centre symbolises Buddha who is surrounded by a number of persons listening attentively. It thus

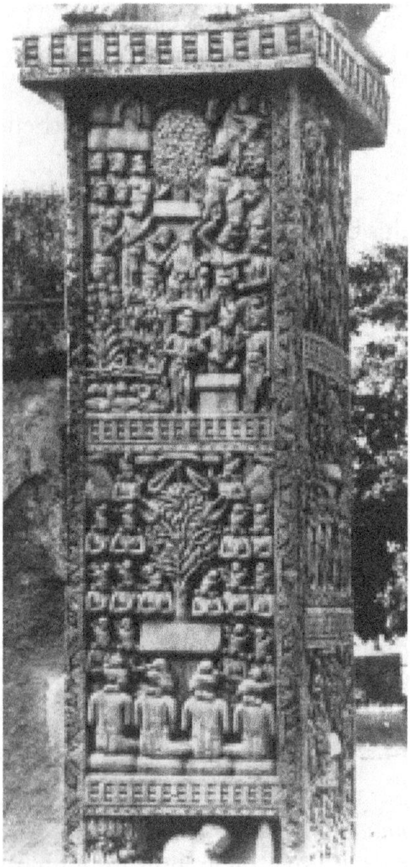

Fig. 3.43 Western Gateway, south pillar, north face

represents the conversion of the Shakyas, the people of his own clan. This scene is also carved on the Northern Gateway.

3. *Dvarapala*

The guardian at the bottom is similar to those on other toranas.

North pillar—north face and south pillar—south face (Fig. 3.44)

The designs carved on the outer surfaces of these pillars are more or less identical. They are among the most charming in the entire range of Indian art. Both pillars have a vertical band inset with animal riders facing opposite directions, and in between them is a lotus creeper which can be identified as the Tree of Life. The animals are vyalas, mythical animals that look like lions, some of them with beak-shaped mouths and some with horns. Incidentally, Ashvaghosha, in his *Buddha-charita*, describes such composite creatures as being part of Mara's army. They include *minashva* (fish horse), *vihangamaksha* (face of a sheep and eyes of a bird) and many others.

Top architrave—front

Trees of Manushi Buddhas (Fig. 3.45)
The seven Manushi Buddhas have been represented by three stupas and four Bodhi trees. The tree on the left of the central stupa is the nyagrodha of Kashyapa and that on the right is the ashvattha of Shakyamuni while that at the right end is the udumbara of Kanakamuni and the corresponding one on the left end may be the shirisha of Krakuchchhanda. They are all flanked by worshippers.

Middle architrave—front

Sermon in the Deer Park (Fig. 3.45)
The central architrave is occupied by the depiction of the first

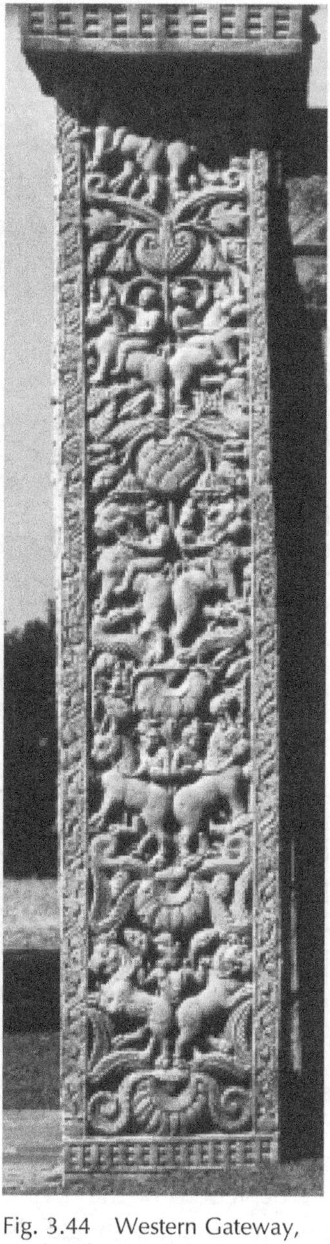

Fig. 3.44 Western Gateway, north pillar, north face and south pillar, south face

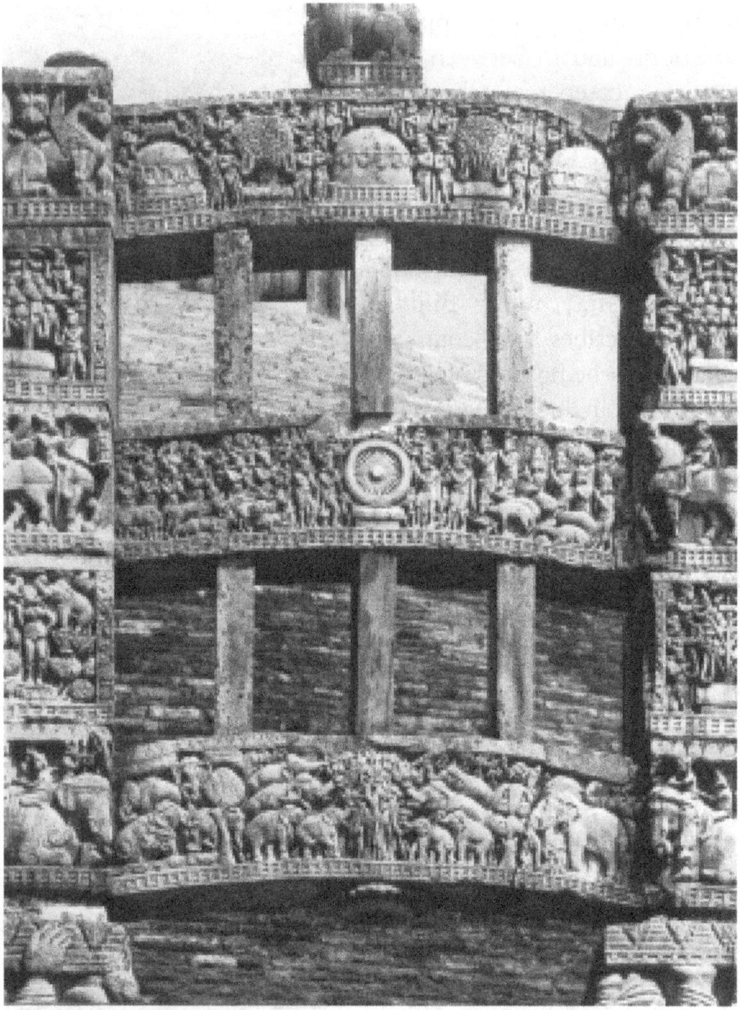

Fig. 3.45 Western Gateway, front, panels on architraves

sermon of Buddha in the Mrigadava (Deer Park) of Sarnath. It is usually marked by a dharma-chakra in the centre on a pedestal, with a number of devotees on either side. But more important are depictions of the deer which were in the park. In fact, the first five disciples should also have been shown; they may be in the crowd, but cannot be identified.

Lowest architrave—front (Fig. 3.45)

The architrave at the bottom is carved with the *Chhaddanta Jataka* which also appears on the Southern Gateway.

On the squarish blocks which slightly project out of the architraves, the usual motifs of Nativity, winged lions, animal riders, bodhi trees, and so on, occur. Of the dharma-chakra crowning the gateway, only the base fragment with the animals supporting it remains.

Top architrave—back

Transport of the relics (Fig. 3.46)
This scene is the same as that on the back of the Southern Gateway, on its lowest architrave. The panel depicts the fight for Buddha's relics which were in the possession of the Mallas of Kushinagara. Armies with elephants, horses, and foot soldiers are surging towards the city gate of Kushinagara which is seen on the left. Just before it is the Bodhi tree. It appears that the person on the elephant is carrying a casket in his right hand.

Middle architrave—back

Siege of Kushinagara (Fig. 3.46)
While the top architrave shows the transport of the relics, on the middle one we see the 'war of the relics', which took place between the Mallas and seven other peoples. The same story is also shown on the Southern Gateway. The composition of the panel is truly remarkable.

Lowest architrave—back

Enlightenment and the defeat of Mara (Fig. 3.46)
This story is also carved on the Northern Gateway. In the centre is a large imposing structure decorated with a chaitya arch and a Bodhi tree emerging out of it at the top. Mara, evil personified, first tried to tempt Buddha by deputing his beautiful daughters and later frightened him with his army of demons, but they were defeated and are all shown running on the right. On the left are worshippers who are happy because of Mara's defeat.

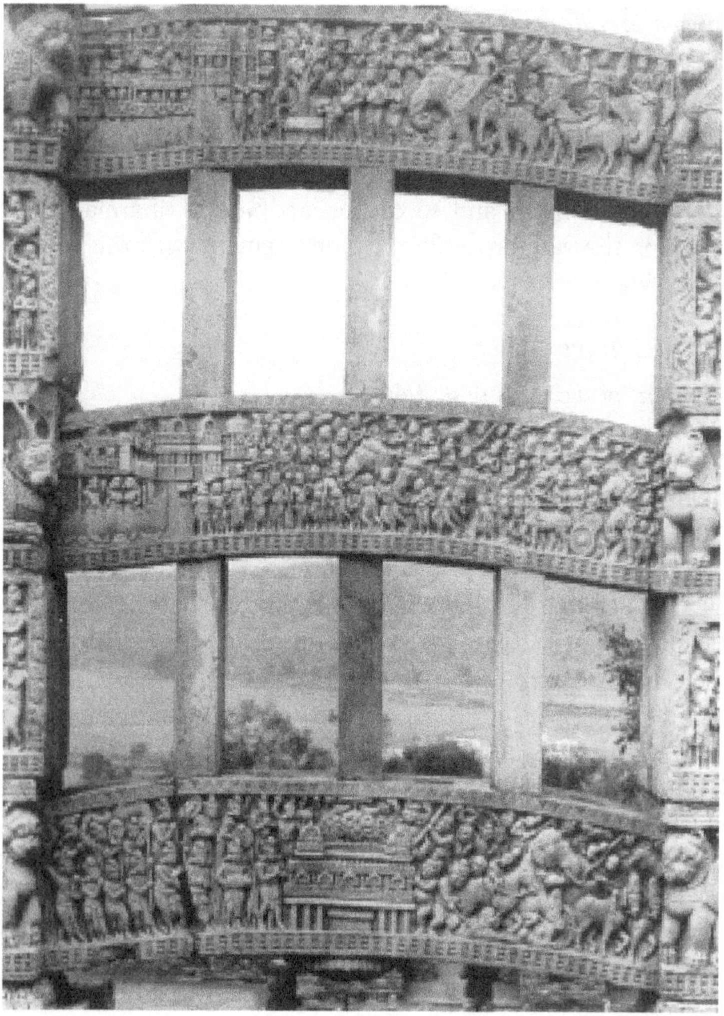

Fig. 3.46 Western Gateway, back

The under surface of the lowest architrave is carved with lotus medallions.

Sculpture

The most important component of the Sanchi monuments is the wealth of carvings on the Gateways (toranas) which constitute the largest and most splendid specimens of not only Buddhist, but the entire range of Indian art (Figs 3.47 and 3.48). They are magnificent examples of structural Buddhist architecture in India. Erecting such toranas was a novel idea, and there is little doubt that such gateways existed in ancient Indian towns, since they are depicted in Sanchi reliefs as well as in a contemporary Ajanta

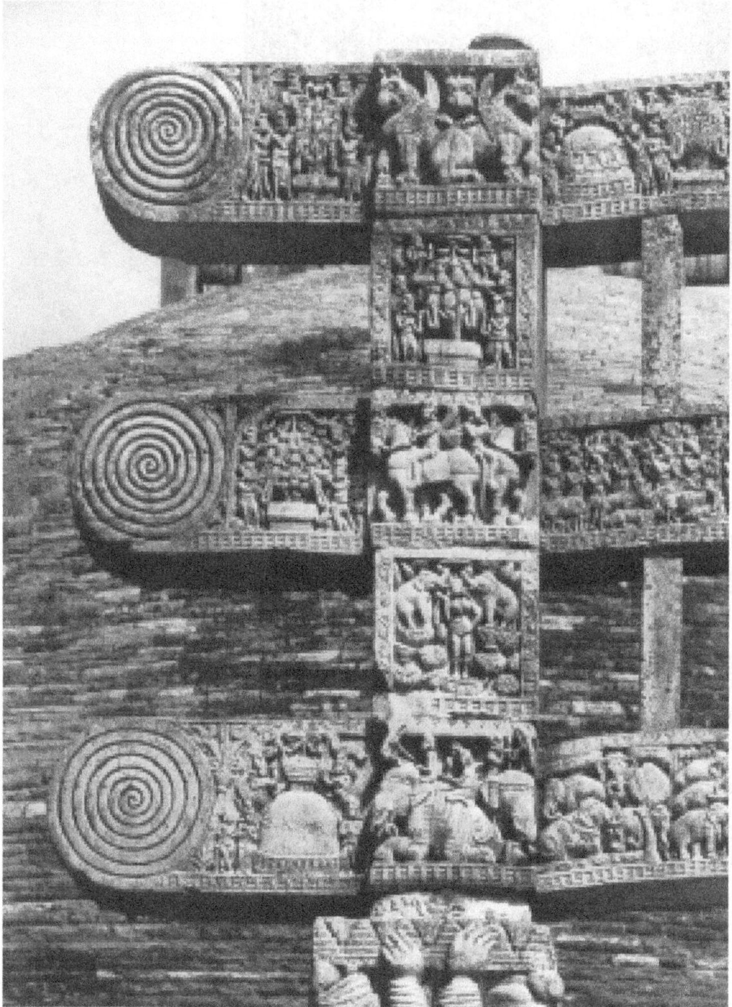

Fig. 3.47 Sculpture motifs

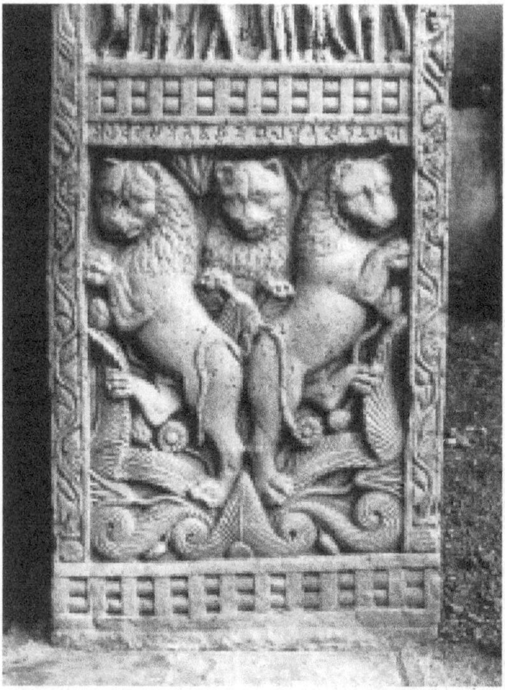

Fig. 3.48 Western Gateway, carving on the south pillar with inscription

painting (Cave 9). Every inch of space on the gateway has been utilised for carving, the aesthetic quality of which is indeed of a high order. It constitutes a running commentary on life in ancient India, for we are shown fortified cities with lofty storied mansions and gateways, huts of hermits, religious structures, armies, and even dense forests with wild animals. These are all treated very sensitively, especially the elephants in the *Chhadanta Jataka*. Nowhere is the balance lost, although all the figures are carved on the same plane. They are marked by the law of frontality and therefore foreshortening or perspective is absent. The carvings are all executed in low relief and they can therefore be better appreciated under light and shade effects.

The stone reliefs give the impression of being wood carvings and it is highly likely that they were the handiwork of wood-carvers. This contention is supported by the inscription of the guild of ivory carvers of Vidisha who state that they have executed some of the reliefs on the Southern Gateway. The finest carvings are those on the Northern Gateway followed by those on the Southern and other gateways. Although all the carvings are more or less contemporary, those on the Eastern and Western Gateways are aesthetically somewhat inferior. This is more evident in the human forms and in such mythical figures as the yakshas and kinnaras. John Marshall observes:

> The Indian artist was adept at executing floral and ornamental pattern; ... Figures are kept in one plane with practically no effort towards spatial effect, and each is portrayed almost as a silhouette, sharply defined against the separate plane of the background, such modelling as there is being effected by rounding the contours of the silhouette or the interior details... They are the work of the artists who were copying direct from nature and were all but free from the trammels of the memory image.

Although Marshall has inferred that these sculptures were the handiwork of artists from northwest India who were influenced by Hellenistic (Greek) art, it is apparent that they are closer in style to the Satavahana sculpture in Western Indian caves, and an inscription on the Southern Gateway even refers to the artist of a Satavahana king. The sculptures are clearly in the Satavahana style and there is no trace of any Hellenistic influence on them.

Inscriptions

Over a thousand inscriptions have been noticed at Sanchi so far though there are probably more, as indicated by the recent discovery of an Ashokan inscription at Satdhara in the Sanchi complex. The ancient Brahmi script was first read by James Princep in 1837, and the Sanchi inscriptions were deciphered by him. Later, in 1854, Alexander Cunningham published many of them. When John Marshall carried out excavations at Sanchi between 1912 and 1919, some more epigraphs were brought to light. These inscriptions are of great value not only for the dating of different monuments, but also because they throw a flood of light on socio-economic conditions in ancient India.

Next to the Ashokan edict, a very important inscription is that on the dome of the central stupa on the Southern Gateway which reads as follows:

rano Siri Satakanisa
avesanisa Vasithiputa
Anamdasa danam

This translates as, 'Gift of Ananda, the son of Vasithi (Vasishthi), the foreman of the artisans (*avasanin*) of King Siri Satakani (Satakarni)'. The king can be identified as Satakarni II of the Satavahana dynasty of the Deccan who ruled in the 1st century BC.

Another inscription on the Southern Gateway reads, '*Vedisakehi dantakarehi rupa-kammam katam*', meaning 'the carving of the sculpture was done by the ivory carvers of Vidisha'. The epigraph is of inestimable value inasmuch as it demonstrates that the ivory carvers were equally adept at working in stone. They carved the 'Siege of Kushinagara' panel on the back of the Southern Gateway (lowest architrave).

Yet another inscription on the south pillar of the Western Gateway records the donation of the pillar by one Balamitra. It reads, '*Aya-chudasa atevasino Balamitrasa dana thabho*', meaning 'the gift of a pillar by Balamitra, a pupil of Ayachuda (Arya-Kshudra)' (Fig. 3.46).

A vast majority of donors at Sanchi were lay worshippers (*upasakas*) while some were monks and nuns who, in several cases, refer to themselves as disciples of particular teachers. Most of the donors are from Malwa, the region in which Sanchi is located, but there are a few from as far east as Magadh (Bihar) and as far south as Paithan (Aurangabad District, Maharashtra) which is identified with ancient Pratishthan, the capital of the Satavahanas. Bhogavardhana is the same as the present Bhokardan (Aurangabad District, Maharashtra) which was an important commercial town and a manufacturing centre.

ASHOKAN PILLAR (No. 10) (Fig. 3.49a)

A noteworthy feature of Mauryan court art, especially of the Ashokan period, is the imposing free standing pillars which the emperor erected at different places in his empire. He had set up one such pillar at Sanchi near the Southern Gateway of the Great Stupa. It was 12.6 m high, with a tapering monolithic shaft and a bell-shaped capital surmounted by four addorsed, majestic lions which in all probability signify the Buddha himself since he was known as 'Shakya-simha' (the lion of the Shakya clan in which he was born). The pillar consisted of two parts: the monolithic shaft, the stump of which is *in situ*; and the lion capital, which is exhibited in the museum. Like other Ashokan pillars, it is made of buff-greyish, extremely fine-grained sandstone which was quarried from Chunar in Bihar and was transported to Sanchi, some 800 km to the west. It may have been brought on rafts along rivers, first the Ganga, then the Yamuna, and lastly the Betwa which is just a little over 1 km from the site. The pillar bears a mirror-like polish, a characteristic of Mauryan art, and the lions are impressive. The lower portion (2.4 m) is embedded in the ground. The inscription on it has been engraved rather clumsily. The pillar was set up in 254 BC.

The pillar fragments which have been recovered at the site show that an Ashokan edict was engraved on it. Ashokan edicts, among the earliest documents, were ordered by the king to be engraved on pillars. It is, therefore, highly likely that some of the so-called Ashokan pillars may precede the emperor. The Sanchi edict was carved on the pillar which was erected near the Southern Gateway of the Main Stupa (No. 1). Originally it consisted of eight lines, but is somewhat damaged, and from what remains it is clear that its contents are identical with those of the Sarnath edict of Ashoka. It states:

> The (split up) *Sangha*, both of monks and of nuns, has been made one united whole. As long as my (sons) and great grand-sons (shall rule) and the moon and the sun (shall shine), the monk or nun who creates a division in the *Sangha* shall be

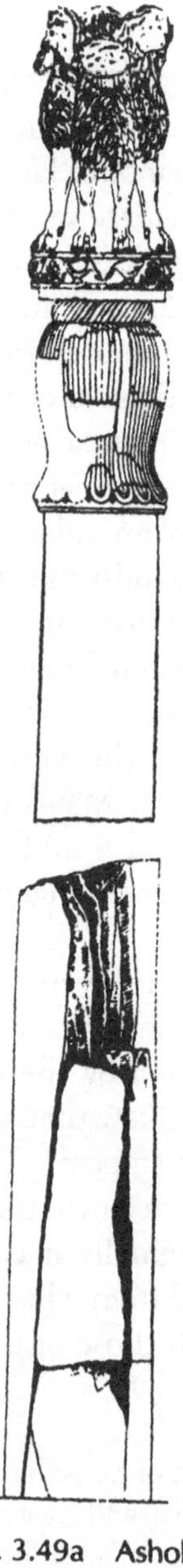

Fig. 3.49a Ashokan pillar

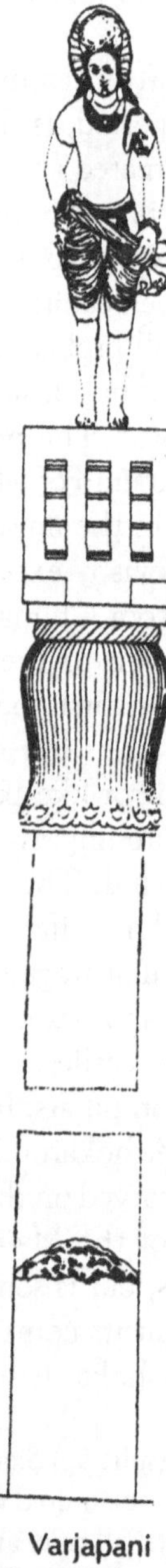

Fig. 3.49b Varjapani pillar, Gupta period, 5th century AD

made to put on white robes and to stay out of the (*Sangha*) residence. For what is my desire?—That the *Sangha* as a united (body) may long endure.

STUPA 3 (Fig. 3.50)

There are some more stupas at the site, though they are of rather modest proportions as compared to the Great Stupa (No. 1). Of these, Nos 3, 4, and 6 are situated on the main terrace. No. 3 is near the northeast corner of the main stupa, about 45 m away, while No. 4 is situated behind No. 3, and No. 6 is near its southeast corner. Only No. 3 has a gateway. Its diameter is 15 m, and its height is 8.1 m; it is crowned with an umbrella (chhatra). In construction it is similar to No. 1 (main Stupa). It was built with stone blocks in its core; the terrace was raised later after the stupa construction was completed. It also had a balustrade, as the bases of pillars which have been traced in the excavation would suggest. It was identical to that of the Great Stupa. The harmika over the stupa and the fragments of its umbrella are also seen.

The stupa was built during the 2nd century BC when the Shungas were ruling over this region as the epigraphical evidence clearly indicates. The inscriptions on relic boxes and the stairway can be assigned to the 2nd century BC on palaeographical grounds. The gateway was added slightly later in the 1st century AD. It was in this stupa that General Cunningham found the relics in the centre of the dome under a large slab of stone (1.5 m long). Inside, there were two stone boxes. On one of these was engraved the name of Sariputta and on the other was Maha-Moggalana; corporeal relics were enshrined in both of them. The box containing the relics of Sariputta was of white stealite (15 cm broad and 7.5 cm high) and was covered by a pottery dish; it contained a small bone fragment, two small pieces of sandalwood, and a few beads of garnet, lapis lazuli, crystal and amethyst, and pearls. Inside was found the letter *sa* (obviously for Sariputta) written in ink. Similarly, the other casket, which was slightly smaller, was marked with the letter *ma*.

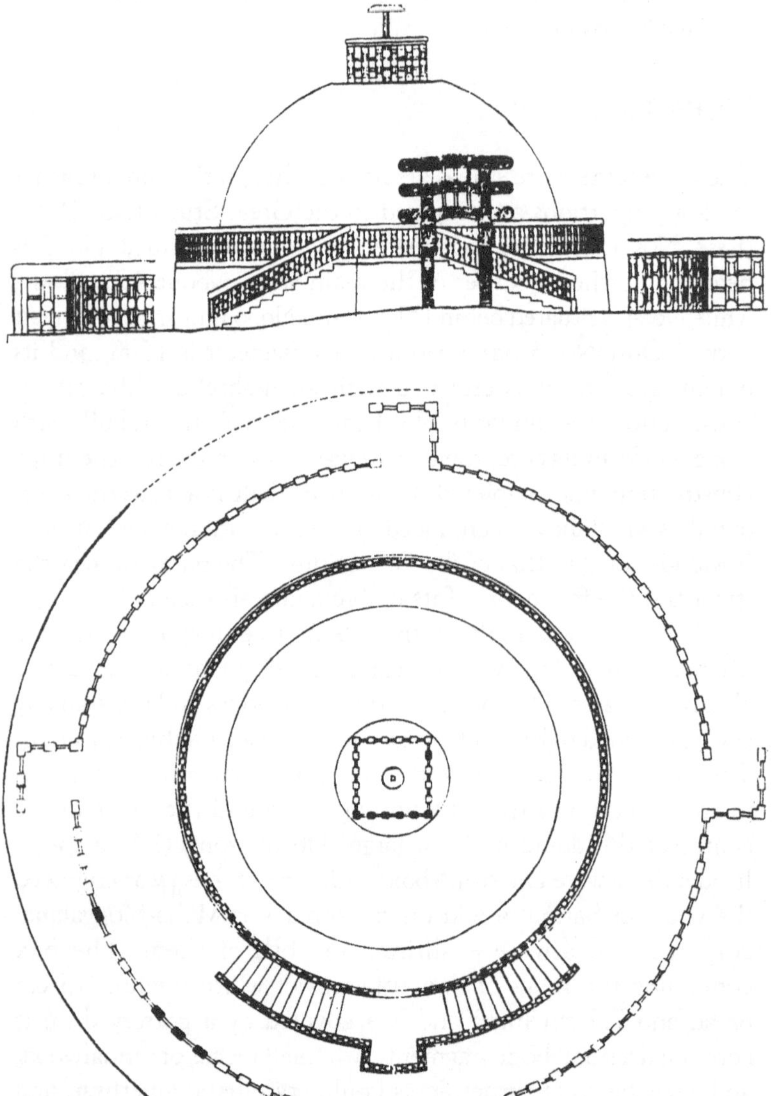

Fig. 3.50 Plan and elevation of Stupa 3

Next to Ananda, Sariputta and Moggalana were Buddha's most favourite disciples, and were therefore highly venerated. They were very close friends and were brahmins. Their relics were enshrined in stupa No. 2 at Satdhara which is about 10 km from Sanchi. It seems that at Mathura too there was a stupa which contained their ashes along with those of others. This has been reported by the celebrated Chinese pilgrims, Fa-Hien (399–411 AD) and Hieun Tsang (629–41 AD) who came to India to visit sacred places associated with Buddha. Of the two, Sariputta, who was more famous, died at Rajagriha (present Rajgir in Bihar) where a stupa was erected over his ashes. It is highly likely that part of the relics were brought to Sanchi. The relics of Sariputta (Sariputra) and Moggalana (Maudgalayana) found at Sanchi (Stupa No. 3), which Cunningham had recovered during clearance, were removed to London.

Stupa 3—Gateway (Fig. 3.51)

The only other stupa at Sanchi that has a gateway is Stupa No. 3. This gateway, like the stupa itself, was in ruins and had to be reconstructed. But in the course of restoration, which was done in the 19th century, it was noticed that the top architrave was not properly placed as the back portion came to the front. This was rectified later. The gateway, however, is smaller than those of the Great Stupa.

The gateway is at a higher level, but in composition and style it is closely related to those of the Great Stupa; its workmanship, however, is inferior. Most of the motifs and scenes are those occurring on the gateways of the Great Stupa; only that of Indra's paradise is different. The crowning sculptures on the uppermost architrave have not survived, and nor have the vertical uprights between the architraves; the figures on the volutes too are absent. At the top of each pillar, both on the front and back, are carved either a stupa with votaries or a dharma-chakra crowning a pillar with a lion capital, whereas in the lower panels we see votaries, three in each row. Only in one case, (west pillar,

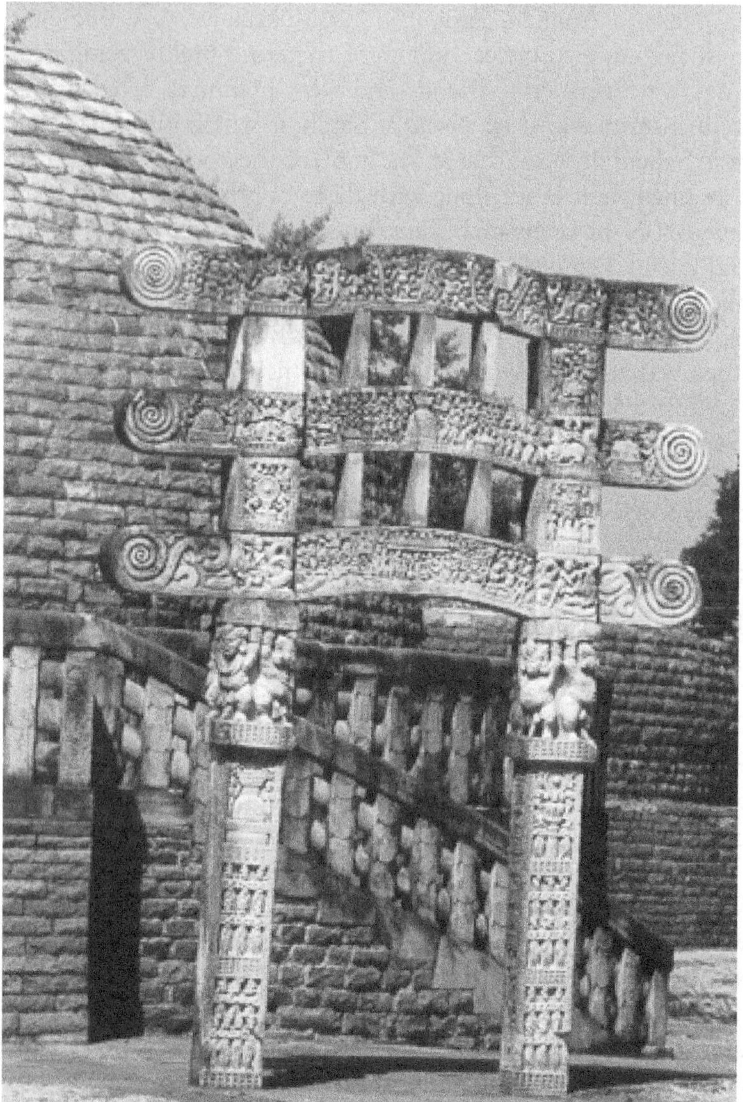

Fig. 3.51 Sculptured Gateway of Stupa 3

north face) there is a Bodhi tree on a high pedestal flanked by worshippers. The east face of the east pillar is adorned with a vertical row of lotus medallions.

The pillars are crowned by four corpulent yakshas standing back to back; they support the architraves above. The top architrave is adorned with a giant creeper with lotus flowers and leaves and in between the curves are dwarfish figures with grotesque features; they are not very different from the demons in Mara's army who are seen on the other gateways of the Great Stupa. On the middle architrave we see a stupa in the centre and two Bodhi trees and there are two more stupas on either end. They seem to represent the Manushi Buddhas.

The lowermost architrave shows what has been identified as the *Nandana-vana*, Indra's paradise, which is the only of its kind at Sanchi. In a spacious hall, Indra is shown seated in the centre accompanied by his paraphernalia, whereas in the upper balcony are women watching the proceedings below. There are rocks and trees and animals such as lions and peacocks too. On either end are Naga-rajas with their consorts and attendants.

The squarish blocks on the sides which slightly project out of the architraves are carved with the usual dharma-chakras, animal riders, stupas, and so on.

OTHER STUPAS

Stupa 4

This stupa is located to the northeast of Stupa No. 3, just behind it, but is completely ruined; what we now see is only a pile of stones. A stone carving, probably a coping stone of the balustrade, was found near the stupa. The stupa dates to the 1st century BC.

Stupa 5

This stupa differs from others in that it is built over a circular plinth (diameter 11.7 m) and not a squarish one as in other cases. On its southern side there is a seated Buddha image in meditating posture (dhyana-mudra); it is fixed on a pedestal. Stylistically, the stupa can be assigned to the 6th century AD.

Stupa 6

Located a little to the east of Temple 18, this stupa was originally constructed in the 2nd century BC but was heavily repaired in the 7th–8th centuries AD. Its core consists of heavy stone blocks and it stands on a square plinth (11.85 sq. and 1.6 m high).

Stupa 7

This is near the southwestern corner of the plateau.

Stupas 12–16 are arranged in two rows near Temple 17. They are all similar in shape and construction. They stand on square plinths which are constructed of stone rubble set in mud mortar. Most of them are solid but some have a small relic chamber in the centre.

Stupa 12

The relic chamber of this stupa was destroyed. The pedestal of a Bodhisattva image datable to the 1st–2nd centuries AD, as is evident from its Kushan workmanship, was found here. The inscription on the pedestal records that this statue of Bodhisattva Maitreya was dedicated by the daughter of one Vishakula. The statue was made of the red mottled sand-stone of Mathura.

There is yet another Buddha statue, carved in the typical red sandstone of Mathura, but assignable to the 5th century AD as is clear from its Gupta style. It was found in Stupa No. 14. Curiously enough, Buddha statues were buried in the Stupas at Sanchi. It is therefore highly likely that this Gupta period Buddha image, seated in meditating posture, may have come from a 5th century AD stupa and was installed later in the 7th century AD.

Stupas 28–29

These small stupas, which may be of votive nature, are situated near Temple 31. They stand on a high squarish base and can be assigned to the Gupta period (5th century AD). There was a relic chamber in Stupa No. 29 which yielded a small receptacle-like clay reliquary, and another similar cup placed over it to serve as a lid. In it was found a small piece of bone and a fragment of a pot which may date to the 3rd–2nd centuries BC. The pedestal of a Buddha statue, of Mathura red sandstone, was also found here. The inscription on it records that 'this statue of Bhagavat Shakyamuni (i.e. Buddha) was installed by one Vidyamati in the 22nd regnal year of King Vaskushana'.

PILLARS

A very interesting feature of the monuments at Sanchi is that there are many free-standing pillars in the complex. The most important among these is the Ashokan pillar which we have already described (see pp. 83–85). Other pillars belong to different periods but almost all of them are broken. They occupy an important position as is clear from the one at Vidisha, which is known as the Heliodorus pillar and also as *Garuda-dhvaja* (with an eagle capital) which was erected in the courtyard of the Vishnu temple.

Pillar 26

Situated to the north of the above, this pillar is made of two pieces, the base being square and the shaft circular. It is 6.75 m high. It had a bell-shaped capital and is crowned by a lion and dharma-chakra (the Wheel of Law). The inscription on the pillar states that the Vajrapani pillar, two pillars of a gateway, the hall (*mandapa*) of a monastery, and a gateway were donated by one Rudrasena or Rudrasimha, son of Goshura Simhabala, who was the superintendent of the monastery. Stylistically and palaeographically the pillar belongs to the Gupta period (5th century AD).

Pillar 35 (Fig. 3.49b)

This is situated near the northern gateway of Stupa No. 1. The pillar was earlier taken to be the contemporary of the Ashokan pillar near the Southern Gateway and was dated to the 3rd century BC, but it is now clear that stylistically it can be assigned to the

Gupta age (5th century AD). At the base of its shaft iron chisels were found. It is also known as the Vajrapani pillar as it is said to have been surmounted by an image of Vajrapani.

Of this massive pillar, only the standing lower portion of the circular shaft, bell-shaped capital, cable necking, the square abacus carved with balustrade in relief lying on the ground, and the crowning Vajrapani which is in the Museum (Mus. Cat. No. A 99), have survived. Vajrapani, clad in a short dhoti, wears a jewelled necklace, heavy earrings, bracelets and an elaborate headdress of *kirtimukha* and jewels; he is shown standing with his left hand holding the ends of his scarf. The right hand, which is broken, held a thunderbolt (*vajra*), part of which is still traceable on the right hip. The most important feature of this image is its small halo, pierced with 12 holes evenly distributed along the margin and evidently intended for receiving the tenons of a metal halo.

Pillar 34

This pillar has totally vanished but for some fragments which are *in situ.*

Pillar 10

Ashokan pillar—see pp. 83–85.

Pillar 25

This pillar is located close to Stupa No. 5, on its south. It is 4.6 m high and its shaft is octagonal below and sixteen sided above. Its bell-shaped capital is surmounted by a square abacus carved with balustrade in relief, but the crowning motif has vanished. Stylistically the pillar belongs to the Shunga period (2nd century BC), but the inscription on it can be assigned to the 5th century AD on grounds of palaeography.

TEMPLES

There are some temples at Sanchi as well which were constructed in different periods starting from the 2nd century BC. Early structural temples in India belong to the Shunga period (2nd century BC). They were mostly apsidal in plan, but squarish temples started to be built in the Gupta period from the 5th century AD onwards. Before the beginning of the Christian era, the adherents of the Hinayana sect of Buddhism did not worship Buddha in human form, but when Buddha images began to be made in the 1st–2nd centuries AD, Buddhist temples enshrining Buddha images were built. There is not much difference in the plans of Hindu and Buddhist temples; it is only the image in the sanctum sanctorum (*garbha-griha*) which marks the difference.

Temple 18 (Figs 3.52 and 3.54)

This is the earliest and the most important of the temples at Sanchi. It must have been an imposing structure when complete but presently only its skeleton (with pillars) is standing. Located just opposite the Southern Gateway, it is built on a raised platform and is apsidal in plan like Buddhist rock-cut temples such as those at Bhaja and Karla. The pillars are inordinately high (5.18 m) in relation to the total size and they rest on stone foundations. They have a square shaft which tapers in the upper part, and are surmounted by a two-armed capital which supports the beam. They are severely plain but for the leaf-shaped medallion carved in the upper part. The inner doorway, which is a later addition, is adorned with male and female figures; the latter stands on a crocodile (*makara*) and can therefore be identified as Ganga. It was added in the 10th–11th centuries AD and is now in the museum. In the apsidal end was a mediaeval stupa which was opened in the 19th century. It yielded a stealite vase which contained relics of some venerable Buddhist monk. The floor of the hall is paved with stones. At the entrance of the temple is a semi-circular moon stone (*chandrashila*). The excavation yielded 56 votive terracotta tablets stamped with Buddha shown seated

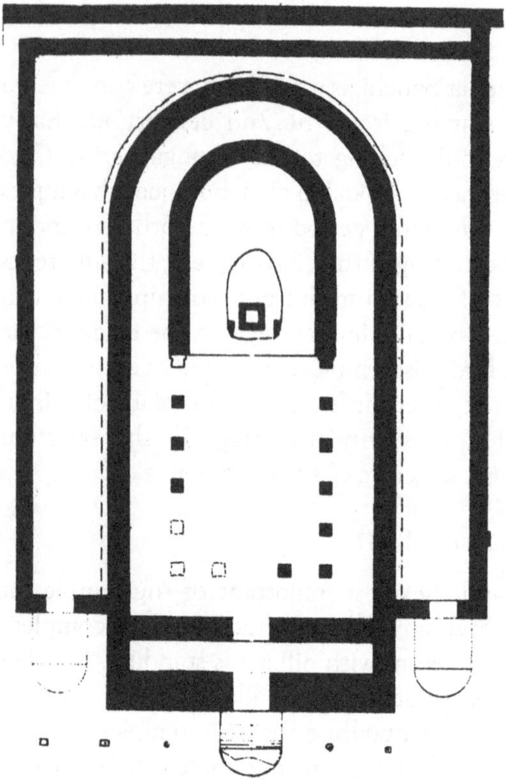

Fig. 3.52 Plan of Temple 18

and touching the earth with his right hand (*bhumi-sparsha-mudra*). He is flanked by a miniature stupa on either side and is inscribed with the typical Buddhist formula '*Ye dharma hetu-prabhava hetum tesham Tathagato-hy-avadatu tesham cha yo nirodha evamvadi maha-sramanah*', meaning 'Of these things (conditions) which spring from a cause, the cause has been told by Tathagata; and their suppression likewise the great Sramana has revealed'. Stylistically, the tablets belong to the 7th–8th centuries AD.

It is evident that the temple belongs to a very early date and additions were made to it from time to time. The three different floors of the temple belonging to the Mauryan, Shunga and late Gupta periods indicate that the original temple was first built in the Mauryan period and is thus contemporary with the Great

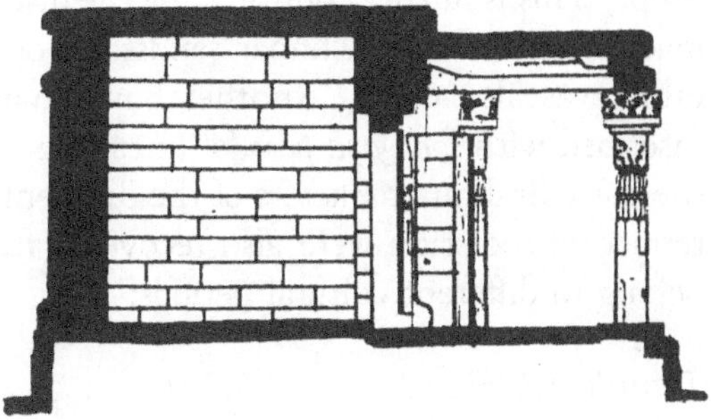

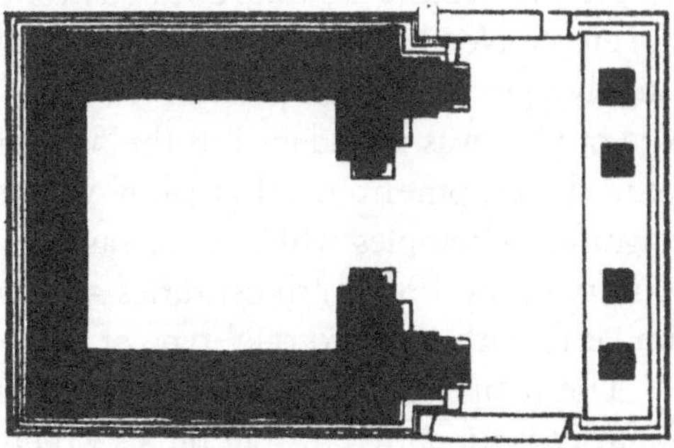

Fig. 3.53 Plan of Temple 17

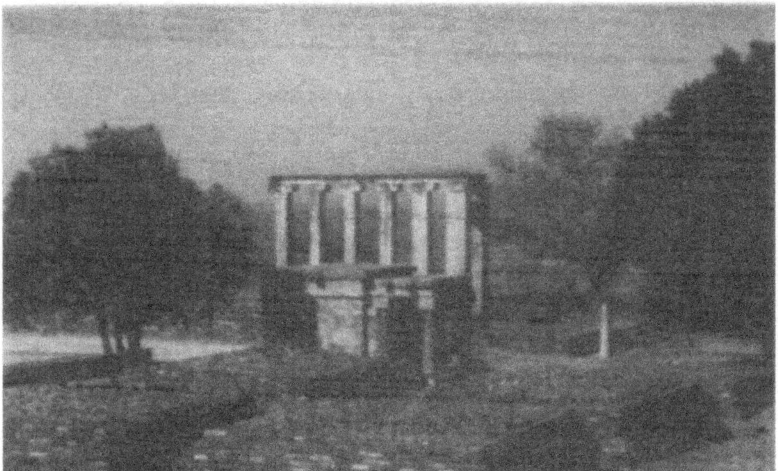

Fig. 3.54 Temples 17 and 18

Stupa. This is further confirmed by the discovery of a stone bowl made of the typical Chunar sandstone of which the Ashokan pillar was also made. Another bowl that was recovered was inscribed with '*bhagaya pasado*' (meaning 'the gift of Bhaga') in the early Brahmi characters of the 3rd century BC. A number of terracotta roof tiles were also recovered from the temple; they belong to different cultural periods.

Temple 17 (Figs 3.53 and 3.54)

This temple is important from the standpoint of the history of temple architecture in India. Located near the northeastern corner of Temple No. 19, it is built on a low moulded basement and is roughly squarish in plan (3.85 m × 3.72 m and 3.9 m high). This type of plan was introduced in the 5th century AD, and it is the later development of this plan which culminates in the magnificent temples which were built in different parts of the country in the 10th–12th centuries AD. The plan bears a striking similarity with the 'prostyle' type of early Greek temples.

The temple is flat roofed and the portico (3 m × 1.8 m) at the front is supported by four pillars which have a square shaft in the lower part, changing into eight and sixteen sides in the middle. Above, it has a bell-shaped top which is crowned with a lion capital; the lions are addorsed and have eight bodies with four heads. The entrance doorway is embellished with a dainty floral pattern. The pilasters on the door jambs are similar to the portico pillars but had, in addition, loose Ganga and Yamuna images. These river goddesses begin to appear on temple doorways from the Gupta period (5th century AD) and also continue later. Presently, there is no image in the shrine, but Maisey, a 19th-century explorer, is reported to have noticed a Buddha image seated on a lotus throne supported by lions and inscribed with the Buddhist *mantra* in characters of the early mediaeval period. But this image obviously was a later addition for the simple reason that on the basis of its architectural style the temple can be assigned to the 5th century AD—a date also supported by the sculptural ornamentation.

Temple 9

Situated near the northwestern corner of Temple No. 18, nothing remains of this temple now, save the plinth of the shrine and the portico. Its plan shows its similarity with Temple No. 17 and it can therefore be dated to the Gupta period (5th century AD).

Temple 31

Located behind Stupa No. 5 in its northeast corner, this temple consists of a plain, pillared chamber with a flat roof. A flight of steps leads to a high plinth which belongs to an earlier temple that stood here in the 6th century AD. Only two pillars standing in the middle belong to the earlier temple. Mention should also be made of a beautiful *nagini* statue of the 5th century AD which was found on the platform of the temple. It is now kept on the southern side of the platform. There is a Buddha image seated on a lotus with an intricately carved halo (*prabha-valaya*) at the back. The present temple was built in the 10th–11th centuries AD.

RETAINING WALL

The high retaining wall was built in the 10th–11th centuries AD.

FOUR

Eastern Area

There are quite a few important monuments in the eastern area. They are located on a slightly higher plateau, with a staircase leading to it, opposite the Eastern Gateway of the Great Stupa.

MONASTERIES 46 AND 47

The track from the steps leads straight to these two monasteries which are located in front of Temple No. 45. They both have a common courtyard; No. 46 is situated to its east and No. 47 to the west of it. It actually seems to be one monastic complex which was constructed in the 11th century AD over an earlier one belonging to the Gupta period (6th century AD). No. 47 is larger (30.9×24.4 m) and consists of a pillared verandah with a small cell and a long narrow chamber at the back. Attached to it on the west is a long pillared chamber, and to its north is a pillared verandah leading into an antechamber and a shrine on the western end. At the back is a corridor with five cells.

Monastery No. 47, situated at a higher level, also has cells on three sides. It is still in a good state of preservation and even its roof has survived in part. Some of the interior walls appear to be later additions. The courts of both the monasteries have been paved with thick stone slabs. The clearance in this area yielded a number of sculpture fragments and carvings, the earliest of which belong to the Gupta period (5th–6th centuries AD), and to which period the earlier structure beneath the present one can also be assigned.

BUILDINGS 49, 50 AND 32

Building No. 49 was a small structure, located to the north of Monastery No. 47, but nothing except its plinth has survived. Building No. 50 was probably a monastery as the few remains, such as the pavement and the stumps of columns, would suggest. It was a contemporary of Monastery No. 47 and is therefore placed in the 11th century AD. But the small shrine in this complex is somewhat better preserved (Building No. 32). It is built at about 3 m above ground level and consists of three small rooms with an antechamber in front. There is also an underground chamber below the central cell which is now covered. There is an entrance in the eastern side of the antechamber and yet another leading into the central chamber. Surprisingly there are no doorways for going into the side rooms, only windows. These chambers may have been used by monks for meditation.

BUILDING 43

This building, situated to the south of Monastery No. 47, is partly built at a higher level on the eastern plateau and on a lower level in the south. It is a massive structure which Marshall compares with the stupa built at Peshawar by Kanishka as it is cruciform in plan with round bastions at its four corners. It is among the latest structures built at the site. The excavation within the enclosed area brought to light the existence of an early mediaeval Buddhist monastery dating to the 7th–8th centuries AD but the structure with bastions belongs to the 11th–12th centuries AD.

TEMPLE AND MONASTERY 45 (FIG. 4.1)

This temple is among the last of the buildings which were constructed at the site sometime in the 10th century AD. But there is evidence to show that there was another earlier temple at the same spot which was built in the 8th century AD. It consisted of some shrines and cells for monks which were arranged around an open courtyard in the centre. This temple was destroyed by fire.

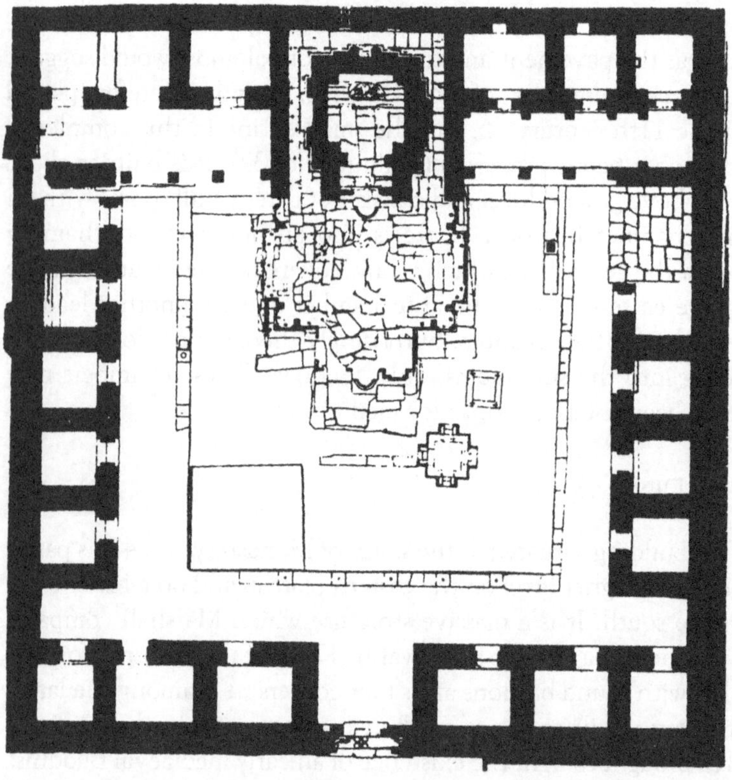

Fig. 4.1 Plan of Temple and Monastery 45

A new temple was built at the site over the remains of the earlier one. A lofty shrine was added, of which the double-storied tower (*shikhara*) is quite impressive. It was built by corbelling, a technique comprising successively diminishing squares which characterises all early Indian temple shikharas. Some carved fragments of the shikhara have been recovered from the debris. The earlier shrine was buried under the new one but the older cells on all the three sides continued to be in use even in the later period; their height was increased and the floor was relaid. Similarly, a new verandah was also added at a level higher than that of the central courtyard.

The later shrine is essentially the sanctum sanctorum (garbha-griha) which is squarish in plan and has a circumambulatory path (pradakshina-patha) around it and a vestibule (*antarala*) at the front. The wall of the sanctum has niches on the exterior, one on each side. The niche in the eastern wall has an image of Buddha in the meditating posture (*dhyana-mudra*) whereas that on the south contains a Bodhisattva who is identified as Vajradharma Lokeshwar, whose mount (*vahana*) is carved below the lotus on which he is seated. It is a rare form of the deity belonging to the Vajrayana sect which developed later in the post-Gupta period. Another image of the same divinity is housed in the museum at the site. It was formerly wrongly identified as that of Mayurvidyaraja, the male counterpart of Mahamayuri, the Buddhist goddess of learning. But there is no such divinity in the Buddhist pantheon and it does not figure in Buddhist iconographical texts.

The shrine doorway has been richly carved with a variety of motifs which very closely resemble those of contemporary Hindu temples. As in the case of Hindu temples, the doorway is flanked by the images of Ganga and Yamuna with female attendants, one of whom is holding an umbrella over the head of the goddess. There is also Kubera with his mongoose or moneybag, and persons holding a conch (*shankha*) and lotus (*padma*). Equally interesting is the *kirti-mukha* resembling a demon's head which is seen in the centre of the threshold. All these motifs occur in Hindu temples and were freely borrowed by the Buddhists. But it is rather surprising that they should also borrow the motif of amorous couples (mithunas) which adorn the door jambs.

Inside the sanctum is an image of Buddha seated in the bhumisparsha-mudra, a position in which he called the earth as witness. He is seated on a double-petalled lotus on which is engraved the usual Buddhist formula in the characters of the 10th century AD. Below is the lion throne (*simhasana*). The halo (*prabha-valaya*) is richly decorated. However, it is doubtful whether this image originally belonged to this temple.

The shrine is flanked by a set of three cells with a verandah. The two cells close to the sanctum have richly decorated but somewhat unfinished doorways. On the left of the antechamber is a huge image of Buddha in meditating posture.

BUILDING 44

This monastery, situated to the south of Temple No. 45, is now survived only by its plinth. It comprised a rectangular hall and an antechamber and was built in the 8th–9th centuries AD. There was probably a stupa in the centre of the hall with cells on either side, but they are too small to serve as residences for monks, and may have been intended for storing images and votive stupas or for meditation as in Building No. 32. In the hall there are two images of Buddha.

FIVE

Southern Area

There are some important buildings in the southern area. While there is no stupa, there is a major temple (No. 40) and a few monasteries (Nos 36, 37, and 38).

TEMPLE 40 (FIG. 5.1)

This is the most important building in the southern group and is also the earliest temple at Sanchi. It is a chaitya of which only the pillars now remain. It was completely buried under debris and was exposed in the excavation. The rectangular stone plinth (26.52 m × 14 m and 3.35 m high) is provided with flights of steps on the east and west. It therefore has two entrances at both ends of the longer side which is rather unusual. But this feature is noticed in some of the caves, particularly Sudama on Barabar Hill (Bihar), which are from the Mauryan period (3rd century BC).

Three different constructional phases of this temple could be discerned in the excavation at the site. The earliest goes back to the Mauryan period (3rd century BC) when the floor was made of rammed clay and the pillars and the roof were wooden. This timber work was later destroyed by fire probably before the middle of the 2nd century BC. It was rebuilt soon after when the stone plinth was enlarged (41.76×27.74 m) and was paved with stones. Octagonal stone pillars were erected, in five rows of ten each, and there were other pillars also as is evident from the fragments recovered from the excavations. There are inscriptions detailing donations on pillars, the palaeography of which shows that they were put up in the 2nd century BC.

The third structural phase is represented by the addition of a structure in the eastern side of the hall. This was done sometime in the 7th–8th centuries AD when the pillars were re-erected; they are square below and octagonal above.

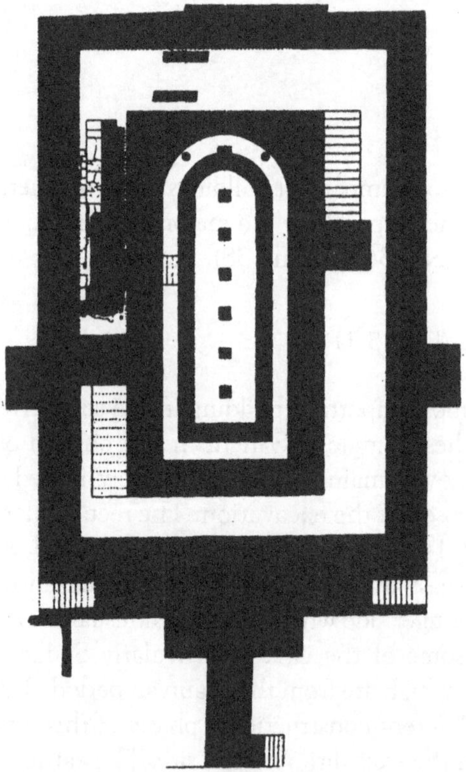

Fig. 5.1 Plan of Temple 40

MONASTERIES 38, 36 AND 37

These three monasteries (Nos 36, 37, and 38) in the southern area were constructed in the mediaeval period.

Monastery 38 (Fig. 5.2)

This is situated in the southeastern corner of the circuit wall and can be approached from Temple No. 40. It was built over an earlier structure of which only the stone foundation survives. It is laid on the usual *chatuhshala* plan, with an open central court with cells on the sides. It was built in the mediaeval period. It also had a compound.

Monastery 36

Of the three monasteries, this seems to be the earliest as it is located near the centre of the site. It is built on the usual chatuhshala plan, consisting of a squarish courtyard in the centre with cells disposed around its sides. The central square has a platform of bricks and along its margin is a low wall in which the

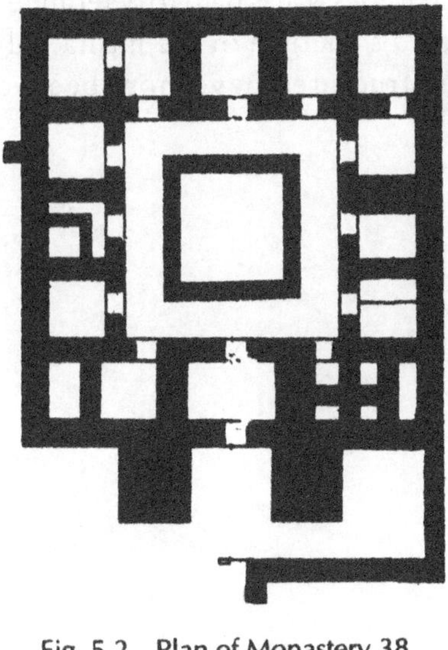

Fig. 5.2 Plan of Monastery 38

pillars of the verandah were erected. The building had an upper storey—as the staircase in the north-western corner indicates. The entrance to the building was provided on the eastern side. There is evidence of underground drainage for the water that collected in the central court. Corner cells had open passages.

Monastery 37

This monastery is more spacious than the other two in this area and is also better constructed. It is located to the west of Monastery No. 38, and was probably erected in the 7th century AD. It is laid out on the usual chatuhshala plan and has four squarish stone blocks with mortic holes for supporting pillars. More rooms were added on the western and southern sides.

BUILDING 8

Only the plinth of this structure now remains which is some 3.6 m above the bed rock. In the middle of its eastern side is a ramp with a few steps and a chandra-shila at the base. The exact function of this structure, which can be assigned to the Shunga period (2nd–1st centuries BC), is hard to determine. Its southeastern corner was enclosed sometime in the mediaeval period.

Some more structures have now been exposed in the southern area.

SIX

Western Slope

MONASTERY 51

This monastery is built on the usual *chatuhshala* plan which consists of an open quadrangle in the centre with cells for monks disposed around it. It has a verandah on the southern side. The structure is roughly squarish (33.22 m×32.69 m) and is built of stone masonry with an exterior of dressed stones, whereas the inner core is composed of stone rubble. The stone walls are faced with bricks. The twenty two cells are mostly of uniform size, except the central one in the western wall which is larger and has an antechamber (antarala) in the front and may therefore have housed an image of some Buddhist divinity. The roof and the verandah pillars were wooden as is clear from the quantity of charred wood which was encountered in the course of excavation.

To the west of Monastery No. 51, a stone paved path leads to Stupa No. 52. On the way is a huge monolithic stone bowl, 2 m high, with a diameter of 1.2 m. A fragment of it has fallen down by its side.

STUPA 2 (FIG. 6.1)

On the western slope of the hill, a pathway leads to Stupa No. 2. The pathway is ancient and is flanked by monuments, the most noteworthy among which is an apsidal shrine. Another building is the imposing Monastery No. 51 which is built on a ledge of the rock.

This stupa, too, is built on an artificial terrace and is similar to Stupa No. 3 in construction and design, but does not have the ornamental gateway which the latter has. It was virtually destroyed by Captain Johnson who excavated it in 1822. He wanted to open it but in the process of his digging demolished it considerably, and whatever survived his vandalism was further destroyed by Alexander Cunningham. Cunningham was a Major-General in the British Army and was deeply interested in India's heritage, but was not a skilled excavator. The stupa has been reconstructed but has lost many of its relief features, and some of the remains, for instance parts of the balustrade and carved members, are now deposited in the site Museum. However, the ground balustrade with four entrances is preserved. The stupa is approached by a double stairway facing the east.

In the course of excavations the relic chamber was found, not in the centre of the stupa, but some 60 cm west of it and at a height of 2.13 m. above the raised terrace. The relic box was carved in white sandstone; it measures 28×19 cm, and the height is 19 cm. Inside it were found four small steatite caskets, each of which contained fragments of bones, while on the relic box was an inscription in early Brahmi characters. It reads:

Savina vinayakana aram Kasapa-gotam upadaya aram cha Vachhi-Suvijayatam vinayaka

"–(The relics) of all teachers including, with the *arhat* (?), Kasapagota and the *arhat* (?) Vachhi Suvijayata, the teacher".

The lids of the four small caskets were also inscribed with the names of ten Buddhist saints and teachers whose ashes were enshrined in the casket.

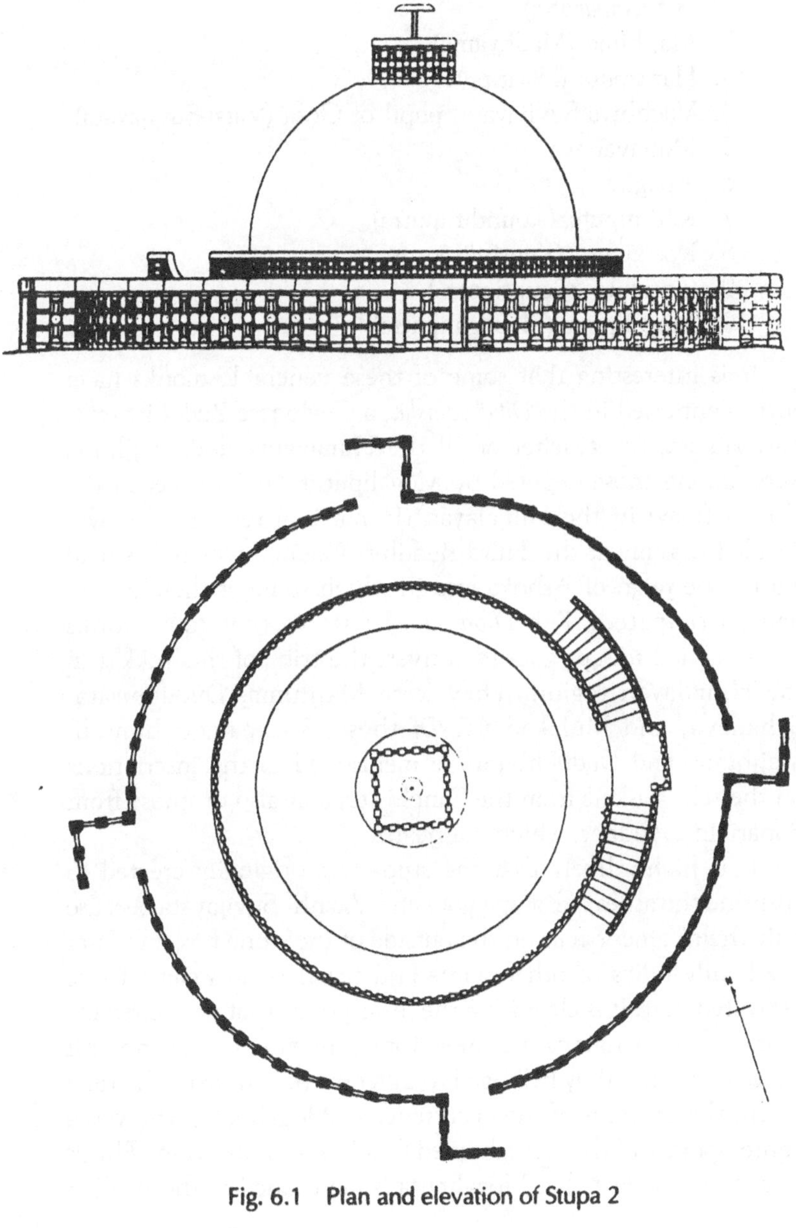

Fig. 6.1 Plan and elevation of Stupa 2

Their names are :

1. Kasapa-gota, the teacher of all the Hemavatas (*Kashyapagotra*)
2. Majjhima (Madhyama)
3. Haritiputa (Haritiputra)
4. Vachhiya-Suvijayata, pupil of Gota (Vatsi-Suvijayata)
5. Mahavanaya
6. Apagira
7. Kodiniputa (Koundiniputra)
8. Kosikiputa (Kaushikiputra)
9. Gotiputa (Gauptiputra)
10. Mogaliputa (Maudgaliputra)

It is interesting that some of these venerable monks have been mentioned in the *Dipa-vamsha*, a Ceylonese Buddhist text. Kasapa-gota, the teacher of all the Himavatas, and Majjhima were among those deputed by Mogaliputta Tissa to preach the *dharma* (Law) in the Himalayan (Hemavata) region. This was decided possibly at the Third Buddhist Council which was held during the reign of Ashoka and in which some of these monks had participated. The *Dipa-vamsha* states that four monks accompanied Kasapa-gota to convert the tribe of the Yakkas in the Himalayan region. They were Majjhima, Dudubhisara, Sahadeva, and Mulakadeva. Of these, Kasapa-gota himself, Majjhima, and Dudubhisara are mentioned in the inscriptions on the relic caskets from the Sanchi stupa as also on those from Sonari and Andher, which are nearby.

It is highly likely that the stupa was originally erected to enshrine the ashes of Kasapa-gota and Vachhi-Suvijayata because only their names occur on the outside of the stone box, but later the bodily relics of other saints and teachers also came to be deposited in it. It is clear from the inscriptions that the venerable monks whose names are mentioned in them were not all contemporaries; they belonged to different periods from the time of Buddha onwards, if the occurrence of Mogaliputa, who was a contemporary of the 'Enlightened One', is an indication. This is clear from the fact that Mogaliputa is mentioned in the Andher and Sonari casket inscriptions as a pupil of Gotiputa. The latter was an heir of Dudubhisara, a colleague of Kasapa-gota and Majjhima in the Himalayan mission. It is therefore clear that the ashes of three generations of Buddhist saints were enshrined in Stupa No. 2. All these reliquaries and the stone box are presently in the British Museum, London. The stupa thus contained the relics of monks who lived between the 6th century BC and the 2nd century BC. It is therefore certain that their ashes were brought from different places and were deposited in the stupa when it was built in the 2nd century BC. It is also not unlikely that the ashes were deposited, when they became available, by opening the chamber in the stupa.

SCULPTURES

The excavation of the stupa brought to light a number of balustrade fragments which are similar to those of the Great Stupa (No. 1), stones carved with a variety of decorative motifs, and sculpture fragments. The predominant motif on the uprights of the vedica rail is the lotus, which is set in a medallion in the centre, with half medallions at the top and the bottom. There are many varieties of the lotus and lotus creepers which, we have seen, is a very common motif at Sanchi. The motifs also include animals such as the bull, horse, elephant, crocodile, deer, cobras and mythical creatures (vyalas), as well as birds such as peacocks and geese. Buddhist motifs such as the tri-ratna, Bodhi tree, and dharma-chakra, which symbolize important events in Buddha's life, also occur. They are shown in combination with plant and animal motifs and also have worshippers flanking them. There are also couples (mithunas), an auspicious symbol connected with fertility. The Nativity scene, which is symbolized by Maya, Buddha's mother, standing or seated on a lotus and being bathed by elephants, is also present.

Although many motifs are repeated, mention should be made of some which have been very exquisitely carved. On one piece is shown Maya, standing on a pedestal with lotus creepers on the sides and elephants bathing her. In the middle is a couple holding hands, and down below is an elephant trampling upon a person. On yet another fragment is the dharma-chakra at the top, over a tri-ratna on a pedestal, which in turn is supported by two yakshas; down below is a couple (perhaps donors) with a child in between them, and at the bottom are two lions. A pillar enclosed by a vedica rail, with a lion capital surmounted by a dharma-chakra, is also noteworthy. There are two prancing deer, facing opposite directions and lotus creepers all around—a very imaginative composition. It is these common motifs which occur in permutations and combinations with other motifs. They are all carved in low relief, akin to the Bharhut carvings, and are therefore assignable to the late 2nd century BC. The stupa itself seems to have been erected a couple of decades after the Great Stupa was constructed.

TANK

To the south-east of Monastery 51 is a large and deep water tank dug into the bed rock. Its shape is irregular.

SEVEN

Museum

There is a site museum at Sanchi which is open daily, except Friday, from 9 am to 5 pm. It contains some of the important antiquities recovered during the excavation of the stupas and is worth a visit. The entry fee is Rs 5. The museum was set up in 1919 by John Marshall, the then Director General of the Archaeological Survey of India. However, as the collections increased the museum was shifted in 1966 to the present building.

Among the important sculptures in the museum mention should be made of the magnificent lion capital of the pillar set up by Ashoka. It is bell-shaped and surmounted by a circular disc-like abacus which in turn is crowned by four lions sitting back to back. It is carved in the typical buff sandstone from Chunar in Bihar. The lions look majestic and their physical features are very carefully carved but unfortunately their heads are broken. The sculpture bears a mirror-like polish which is characteristic of Mauryan art. It is identical to the lion capital at Sarnath. The fragmentary stone umbrella (chhatra) and the stone bowl are also from the Mauryan period. The umbrella must have crowned the brick stupa which was built at the site by Ashoka.

Another important sculpture is the female figure which is clearly a shalabhanjika, similar to those on the Northern Gateway. Unfortunately it is very badly mutilated and only the torso has survived but that too is in a ruined state. It has been placed below a tree as it would have been on the gateway. It obviously must have adorned the Northern Gateway.

There are some interesting Buddha and Bodhisattva images in the Museum which are of much later Gupta and post-Gupta dates. Minor artifacts and objects of daily use which were found in the excavation at the site are also on display.

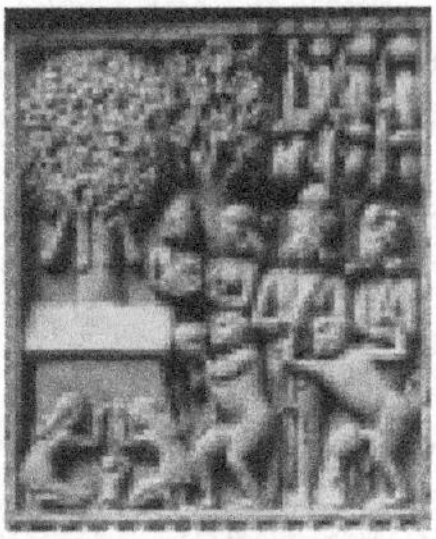

Practical Information

The Buddhist monuments at Sanchi are located in peaceful surroundings on a low hill, not far from the Sanchi railway station. The monuments—stupas, pillars, and monasteries are open from sunrise to 6 pm. Tourists on a short visit can cover in a day Stupas 1, 2, and 3, Temples 17 and 18, and Temple and Monastery 45.

The Site Museum is open daily (except Fridays) from 9 am to 5 pm.

Photography permission

Still photography at the monuments, without tripods, is permitted. For a video camera without a tripod there is a nominal fee. But for using a tripod, both for still photography as well as for video or film shooting, written permission is required from the Director General, Archaeological Survey of India, Janpath, New Delhi 110 001.

Season: The best time to visit Sanchi is between October and March. The monsoon lasts from mid June to September.

How to reach Sanchi: Sanchi is situated 47 km from Bhopal, the capital of Madhya Pradesh, and 9 km southwest of Vidisha. Sanchi has a railway station, but only passenger trains halt at Sanchi, and the Punjab Mail halts only on request by A/C Ist and IInd Class passengers traveling over 161 km. It is advisable to travel from Bhopal, from where taxis and deluxe and ordinary buses to Sanchi are available.

Bhopal is connected by air, rail, and road with many Indian cities.

Air: Daily Indian Airlines flights connect Bhopal to Delhi, Mumbai, and Indore.

Rail: Bhopal is on the route for Express trains from Delhi, Mumbai and Chennai. The superfast Shatabdi Express, connecting Bhopal with Delhi, is a convenient train.

Road: Madhya Pradesh Road Transport runs frequent deluxe and ordinary buses to Sanchi from Hamida Road Bus Stand. Taxis can be hired from Bhopal for a day's trip to Sanchi, Vidisha, and Udaygiri Caves.

Where to Stay:

Sanchi:

MP Tourism: 1. Travellers' Lodge, Tel: 07592–62723.
2. Tourist Cafeteria.

For Booking: State Tourist Officer, Gangotri, 4th Floor, T.T. Nagar, Bhopal, Tel: 0755–554340, Fax: 5774289.

P.W.D. Rest House. Reservation with the Executive Engineer, P.W.D. Vidisha.

Shri Lanka Mahabodhi Society Guest House, near the railway station.

Bhopal: Hotels to suit different budgets are available at Bhopal.

Festivals: Sanchi is still an active centre for the Buddhists. They celebrate the Chaitya-giri Vihara Festival in late November every year when the relics of two of Lord Buddha's early disciples—Sariputta and Maha-Moggallana—are brought out for display. The relics are said to have been discovered in Stupa 3 in 1853 and are kept in the Vihara for the rest of the year.

Places around Sanchi

There are other groups of Buddhist monuments besides the Sanchi complex which are situated in the neighbourhood at Sonari, Satdhara, Pipaliya (Bhojpur) and Andher. They are, however, very plain and without any sculptural embellishment. Recently, one more stupa complex was discovered at Satdhara where an Ashokan inscription was found.

Vidisha

Vidisha, being an ancient capital town, has remains which are worth a visit. The ancient remains of Vidisha lie 8 km north-west of the present town and excavation revealed that it was a flourishing town from the 4th century BC to the 5th century AD. It was earlier the capital of the Akara country and later of Dasharna. It was located on important ancient trade routes joining north and south as well as east and west. A Vishnu temple from the 2nd century BC was uncovered in the course of excavation and an inscribed pillar was also found. The inscription records that it was erected by one Heliodorus, the ambassador of the Indo-Greek ruler Antialcidas to the court of king Bhagabhadra, in the late 2nd century BC. The State Museum, which houses sculptures and artifacts from excavations in the area around Vidisha, is located behind the railway station. Accommodation is available at Vidisha in medium class hotels. Taxis can be hired here to visit Sanchi.

Udayagiri Caves

Udayagiri caves, which are about 9 km from Vidisha, contain exquisite Hindu sculptures of the 5th century AD, in the classic Gupta tradition, carved during the reign of Chandragupta II (380–415 AD). The caves are located about 8 km from the town.

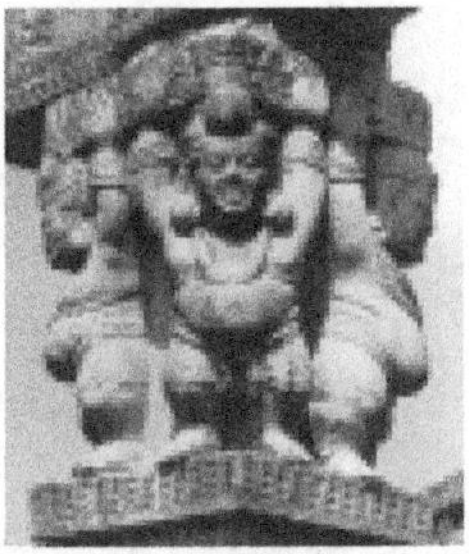

Glossary

architrave:	horizontal member of gateway
Ashta-mangalakas	eight auspicious symbols
Ashvamedha:	horse sacrifice
balustrade:	small pillar supporting hand rail
bhumi-sparsha-mudra:	attitude of touching the earth with right hand
Bodhi tree:	pipal tree (*Ficus religiosa*)
Bodhisattva:	a divinity who has not yet reached Buddhahood
Buddha-pada:	Buddha's feet
chaitya (*chetiya*):	stupa
chakravartin:	universal sovereign/teacher
chankama:	promenade
chaturamaharajika:	Lords of four quarters
chhatra:	umbrella
dagoba (Sk. *dhatu-garbha*):	bodily relics; also domes or stupas enshrining bodily relics
dharma-chakra:	wheel of law

dharma-chakra-pravartana:	turning the wheel of law
dikpala:	Lord of quarter
dvarapala:	usher, guardian
harmika:	a squarish box-like member crowning a stupa
Hinayana:	Buddhist sect which believed in the symbolic worship of Buddha
Jataka:	stories of Buddha's past births
kalpa-vriksha:	wish-fulfilling tree
kalpa-lata:	wish-fulfilling creeper
kinnara:	a mythic creature with a human upper part and a bird-like lower part
kirti-mukha:	dragon-like head
lokapalas:	guardians of quarters
mahabhinishkramana:	Buddha leaving the palace—the Great Departure
maha-janapada:	Great republic
maha-pari-nirvana:	Buddha's death
Mahayana:	Buddhist sect which worshipped Buddha in human form
Maitreya:	future Buddha
Manushi Buddhas:	human Buddhas
Mrigadava:	Deer park at Sarnath near Varanasi
naga:	cobra, worshipped as a deity; also elephant (Sk.)
nagini:	female cobra, worshipped as a deity
Nativity:	Buddha's birth
prabha-valaya:	halo
pradakshina-patha:	circumambulatory path
shalabhanjika:	young damsel clinging to a tree
simhasana:	lion throne
stupa:	originally a funeral mound or tumulus, but later enshrining the ashes of Buddha or some venerable Buddhist monk. It consists of a cylindrical base with domical top
suchi:	cross bar

torana:	gateway
tri-ratna:	Buddha, *dharma* (law, religion) and *sangha* (monastic order)
Tryastrimsha:	Heaven of Thirty-Three Gods
ushnisha:	coping stone
vedica:	railing pattern
volute:	spiral
vriksha-chaitya:	shrine of Bodhi tree
vyala:	a mythical composite creature
yaksha:	semi-divine male
yakshi:	semi-divine female

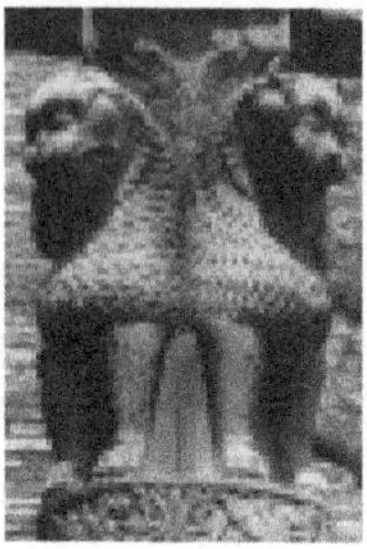

Further Reading

It is surprising that although Sanchi is one of the most important monuments, not much has been written on it—the reason being that John Marshall's work is so thorough and comprehensive that there is not much scope for others. Sanchi figures in every book on Indian art.

Dhavalikar, M.K., *Sanchi—A Cultural Study* (Pune 1965, reprinted 1997).

Maisey, F.C., *Sanchi and Its Remains* (London, 1892).

Marshall, John, *Catalogue of Museum of Archaeology at Sanchi, Bhopal State* (Calcutta 1922).

Marshall, John, *A Guide to Sanchi* (Delhi, 1955).

Marshall, John, Foucher, Alfred, and Majumdar, N.G., *The Monuments of Sanchi*, 3 vols. (Delhi, 1940).

(The original volumes are of inordinately large size and difficult to handle, but they have now been reproduced in a smaller handy size by Swati Publication, Delhi in 1982 and 1983).

Nath N., and Saxena, J.P., *Archaeological Museum of Sanchi* (ASI, New Delhi, 1966).